The Last Fish War
Survival on the Rivers

By Lawney L. Reyes
Edited by Therese Kennedy Johns

CHIN MUSIC
P R E S S

2016
CHIN MUSIC PRESS, *PUBLISHERS*
SEATTLE

PUBLISHER:
Chin Music Press Inc.
1501 Pike Place #329
Seattle, WA 98101
USA

http://chinmusicpress.com

First [1] edition

isbn: 978-1-63405-002-9

COVER PHOTOGRAPH: The Post Intelligencer Collection,
Museum of History & Industry
COVER DESIGN: Mallory Jennings
MAP & ILLUSTRATIONS: Lawney Reyes

ALSO BY THE AUTHOR
White Grizzly Bear's Legacy: Learning to Be Indian
B Street: The Notorious Playground of Coulee Dam
Bernie Whitebear: An Urban Indian's Quest for Justice

Dedicated to the Chinook, the Coho, the Chum, the Humpback

Table of Contents

Preface

OVER THE YEARS, I became fully aware of the injustice, hard times, prejudice and the abuse suffered by members of the Puyallup and Nisqually tribes. I learned this first hand when I fished with Bob Satiacum in 1957 on the Puyallup River and Commencement Bay, near the city of Tacoma. During that time I experienced the arrogance of the white Sportsmen and law enforcement authorities in the area. I witnessed the harsh treatment dealt to the small body of natives who were simply trying to survive.

Because of what I learned in those days I decided to put into print those difficult times. I felt it important to let the overall public understand the truth of what a small band of natives endured to receive justice, not only for themselves, but for their entire tribes. They coped with this harsh treatment by going underground, hiding from the authorities, much like criminals who had broken the law. But all knew they were not the law-breakers. In truth, it was the authorities who were breaking the law, the laws they invented.

During those difficult times I met selfless, but courageous people, who would not bend to the wishes of the dominant authority, people who became my friends. Over time, I got to know intimately those stalwarts: Bob Satiacum, Billy Frank Jr., Clifford Mowich, Hank Adams, Al and Maiselle Bridges and their daughters, Valerie, Suzanne, and Allison, and finally, my brother, Bernard Reyes (Bernie Whitebear).

When up against forces beyond your control, you appreciate the importance of "comrades in arms." You learn that in order to survive you must rely and trust those fighting beside you.

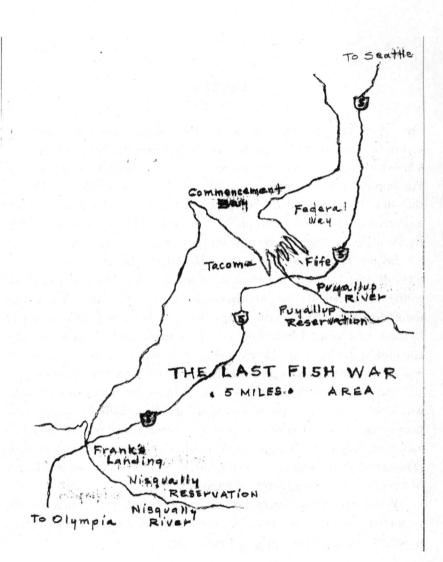

THE LAST FISH WAR AREA
• 5 MILES •

"Before the invasion by foreigners, all beings on the North-American continent worshipped their mother earth and were in tune and at peace with themselves and their environment. There were rules that all understood and lived by. The land the water, and all that lived were respected and cherished. It was God-given and looked upon as a paradise."
– Lawney Reyes (Sin Aikst)

Genesis

FOR CENTURIES, the Indian tribes along the Washington coast lived in a quiet and peaceful manner. There was no need for competition or conquest. No one needed to hoard or challenge others for food, land or other possessions. There was enough room for everyone to live in their own way as they chose. There was no dissention or animosity among the tribes, and they respected each other's presence and way of life. In some cases, marriages took place, welding the relationships of certain tribes closer together. When other tribes pursued different ways or beliefs, it was accepted and respected by everyone.

In 1833, Dr. William Fraser Tolmie arrived in the Puyallup area from Fort Vancouver. He had traveled the Cowlitz River by canoe and overland by horseback. Tolmie was born in Inverness, Scotland, and at the age of twenty received a medical degree from the University of Glasgow. After arriving in the Tacoma area, he viewed what is now called Mt. Rainier and expressed desires to see it closer. He chose Lachalet, a Nisqually Indian, and Nuckalkat, a Puyallup, to guide him there. Later, he was appointed Chief Factor of the Hudson Bay Company at Fort Nisqually and served there until 1859.

When Tolmie and his small party arrived in the Tacoma area, they observed a number of Indians, native to the area, fishing at the mouth of a river as it flowed into the bay. They were seated in dugout canoes carved from cedar logs. The crafts were simply powered by the flow of the river or at times pointed paddles made of wood. They fished with primitive, handmade nets fastened from narrow, flexible limbs of branches tied with some sort of sinew. While floating on the river, the fishermen laid their nets in a semi-circle alongside their slender canoes. This made it easier to snare salmon when they made their way upriver. Other fishermen used spears with tips of stone or bone.

Tolmie discovered simple dwellings made of split cedar planks along the banks of the river and the bay. They were covered with shed roofs slanted to easily shed the rain. Men, women, and children entered and exited the shelters throughout the day, going about their business. Tolmie observed that the Indians lived in a quiet and orderly way.

The visitors could see that the Indians were mildly curious of their presence. There were no outward manifestations of intolerance. These early visitors felt secure and could see that the area was beautiful as the land related easily to the water about it. A great forest of cedar and fir came up to the shores and spectacular snow-covered mountains glittered in the distance, both to the west and to the east. At times numbers of elk and deer appeared quietly grazing at the edge of the forest, seemingly unmindful of the natives about them. Smaller animals on land and water accompanied them. A large assortment of birds busied themselves in search for food. The white men could readily see that this was a special place, a paradise.

Later, more white settlers journeyed to the area searching for places to live. Many faced hardships and danger along the way. They came from different parts of the country, many from east of the Mississippi. When they crossed the plains, a number of tribes, angered by their presence, attacked their wagon trains with intentions of harming and killing. The whites traveled in a land unfamiliar to them. Many made their journey ignorant of what was before them. Most did not know where they would finally make home, but they were determined to find a place, somewhere in the West that suited them.

During those early years, the journey west was beset by numerous hardships that tested the mettle of the thousands who traveled west. The mode of travel was, for the most part, by covered wagon pulled by horses, and sometimes, oxen. The whites learned the journey was perilous and were forced to live off the land. Both large and smaller game, along with fish caught in rivers, streams and lakes, provided much of the food for those who journeyed.

Many encountered various tribes of Indians along the way; some friendly but others hostile. Since many were on a schedule, controlled by weather conditions, there was no time for the whites and the Indians to get to know and understand each other. During those years, negative attitudes were sometimes born and formed by those who journeyed west. At other times when tribes appeared friendly, there was no need to be concerned and wary. But when tribes were unfriendly, fighting occurred, and members of both groups were injured or sometimes killed.

Many whites journeying west had never met Indians. Those from places like New York, Boston, Philadelphia, and other cities along the eastern seaboard had, at best, only read about Indians in newspapers. At times the stories contained negative reports. Many readers began to form opinions that Indians were untrustworthy and dangerous. Others, who were not easily swayed could only express wonder at what they read.

When the travelers reached the large body of water of the sound and the beautifully forested area that lined the shore, they were overwhelmed by the beauty before them. They could see the land was heavily populated by both large and small game. As more whites came, they witnessed large amounts of sea life and abundant runs of salmon in the water. It was at this time they decided to name the great body of water Commencement Bay. It was aptly named because it signified a new start, a beginning for all of them.

Commencement Bay bordered what is now the city of Tacoma to the east and was directly north of the Tide Flats where much of Tacoma's industry exists today. For centuries, a variety of salmon had come from Alaskan waters far to the north, the chinook and the coho becoming the most prized; the chum and the humpback coming a little later in the season. These salmon gathered in great numbers in the Bay to congregate and rest before making their runs into the Puyallup River. The purpose was to go upstream to spawn and create a new cycle of life.

The whites learned this was the beginning of the Indian's season for obtaining salmon. They soon found that salmon was the most important staple for these people; their fishermen spent much time harvesting them and preparing them for immediate and future use. The whites would later learn that the Indians living there were of the Puyallup Tribe. Many wondered how long they had been in the area. Others wondered where they came from, not realizing they were there for centuries.

Over time, more whites made their way to the newly discovered land to find a new life. Like those before them, they were greatly impressed with the area. They loved how it related to the great bay of water. The snow-capped mountains, in the distance to the east, echoed the mountains to the west, and awed everyone. A great mountain, standing majestically, could be seen to the southeast. The beauty of this magnificent snow-capped peak continued to hold many spellbound.

During the mid 1800s, others arrived and were confident that they made the right choice in selecting this part of the country to settle and make their homes. In time, their small settlements grew, forged together, and became the city of Tacoma.

During this time the new settlers again observed the natives who lived in the area. They could see they were tolerant but they kept their distance. The settlers soon occupied themselves in the business of building shelters and other small communities. The Indians were ever curious of the large number of newcomers moving in. Soon they became concerned as they began to settle on the land they had always used. Slowly the natives adjusted to the presence of the newcomers and went about their business of living as they always had and fishing the river and the Bay.

As time went on, the settlers became interested in how the natives fished and maneuvered the river and Bay in their handmade canoes.

They soon learned that the natives were adept at being on the water and expert at catching the great numbers of salmon that seemed to be always present. After the salmon were caught, the settlers became more interested in how they were prepared for eating. They saw that the salmon were skewered by wood stakes that were pushed into the ground forming a circle around a glowing fire. Afterwards, they were slowly roasted to perfection. As they watched, the settlers found the aroma of this process very appealing.

The settlers found interest in the water and soon learned to fish using methods of their own. Some remembered how the natives prepared the salmon and used the same methods after they had made their catch. Others were simply attracted by the beauty of the Bay, and when the weather was pleasant, they spent hours of their leisure boating on the water, enjoying the scenery, visiting with friends and fishing for whatever could be caught. Now Tacoma and the Bay attracted many whites from all walks of life as if by some powerful magnet. Everyone found it was a good place to live and to play.

In those early days, fishing for salmon became an adventure that the whites enjoyed.

For centuries the Bay had been used by the Indians native to the area. Eventually, it became a place of adventure for the whites. Soon fishing these waters became a sport to them. At times, competitions were held to see who could catch the largest salmon.

In time, the number of whites on the water grew, and the natives began to find it difficult to fish in their accustomed way. As years passed, differences arose between the whites and Indians, both on the land and the water. Soon it would become a place of conflict as both sides struggled to control and fish for the salmon that came into the Bay.

The Indians became alarmed as they watched the number of whites continue to grow. They were surprised at the numbers that continued to move in. They observed the whites were in the process of claiming everything that came from the water. Ownership was contradictory to Indian nature, and the action of the whites confused them. The Indians knew that their forebears had lived in the area for centuries and were never challenged in regard to ownership. Soon the interplay of both whites and Indians on the water turned to dissention. From that point on hard feeling against each other grew and became commonplace.

Before the advent of the white man to the Pacific Northwest, the Puyallup Indians were a peaceful people, content to live among themselves and in concert with neighboring tribes like the Nisqually, the Muckleshoot, and the Duwamish, further north. All followed religions that honored the spirits and all had deep respect for their Mother Earth. Those native to the area respected everything living, and there was a balance maintained between all living things. These coastal tribes would gather regularly for their seasonal potlatches located in a variety of places. A popular location was where the Puyallup River drained into the Bay. At certain times of the year, neighboring tribes gathered to enjoy the catch that came from the water and partake of each other's company.

There were never any bad feelings among these tribes. At one time, they were considered among the wealthiest in the nation because of the abundance of food. The salmon runs were believed to be the greatest in the world; there was always enough for everyone.

This began to change when a greater number of whites came with intentions to invade, change, and conquer those native to the land. As they settled, forests were cut down destroying the natural habitat of all wildlife. The deer and elk, finding no place for shelter, disappeared further east to the mountains. This basically put them out of range for the Puyallup; the tribe had to concentrate on food that came from the Puyallup River and the Sound.

As settlements along the Bay expanded and merged, the city of Tacoma grew. As more whites moved in, the Indians of the area found that, year by year, their land base was shrinking. The places they lived were restricted to areas distant from the favorable parts of the growing city. It sobered all Indians when whites continued to push them from the land they loved and force them into areas that no one wanted. All were distraught, then angered, when the whites began to claim everything in the area: the land, the fish, and the water. The natives found it hard to understand that foreigners were taking for themselves all that had been theirs for centuries.

As the white population continued to grow, the Indians learned that the foreigners had passed laws restricting them from fishing on the great Bay itself. They found that whites permitted them to fish only on the Puyallup river bordering the small piece of land where most of them now lived. As time went on, the Puyallup saw that age-old landmarks which were always identified in the Puyallup tongue were being given English names. The descriptions used by the whites seemed meaningless and foreign to the Indians. Later, they learned that their beloved mountain Tahoma, that glowed in the distance, was renamed Mount Rainier.

At that time, the Puyallup Indians did not know that their loss would eventually include their rights and finally their culture itself. It was at this time that the Indians began to learn the real meaning of the word "prejudice."

When examined, prejudice against Indians is somewhat different from that attitude experienced by other minorities. Those who have studied the phenomenon are perplexed. They wonder why the Indians have been faced with the most severe prejudice. Since they were on this continent first and did not come here from distant countries to compete for land and its riches, one might conclude they would be exempt. They had helped the first whites, who landed on the eastern shores of the country, to survive starvation. It seemed this would go in favor of the Indians. Later, if there were any feelings of gratitude by the whites for the Indians, they were soon forgotten.

Unlike the Indians of the Plains, who depended on buffalo and other large game to sustain their lives, the Indian tribes in this area depended on the salmon and other sea life that came from the river and the Bay. During their trip west, the whites learned that the cultures of the Indians they had encountered along the way varied in many ways. The languages were markedly different as well as their dress. The weapons of the tribes varied. The food and ways of obtaining it were not comparable. The tribes of the West Coast were not warlike as were the Indians of the Plains. There was no need for it.

Soon the Indians found they were not welcome in the settlements that were occupied by whites, and exclusion became a way of life for all of them. With the advent of white people in the 1800s, life began to change for the local tribes. The land the Puyallup had always cherished was being encroached upon by an ever-increasing number of light skinned foreigners. As their numbers grew, they found they needed more land to settle in.

In 1854, the Puyallup, the Nisqually, the Muckleshoot, and other tribes that depended on salmon in the area were pressured into ceding about two and a quarter million acres of their land to the United States. Without fully understanding this agreement, the Indians were pushed into The Medicine Creek Treaty by the appointed governor and superintendent of Indian affairs, Isaac Ingalls Stevens.

In 1853, Washington territorial governor and Indian agent, Isaac Stevens, was sent by the president of the United States to negotiate treaties with the Northwest Indians. In truth, his mission was to spread a thin layer of legality over the taking of Indian land.

Stevens, a dwarf of a man, physically and mentally, had no respect for the Indians or whatever rights they pursued. He was anxious to engage in the termination of the Indians' land rights. Not unlike the Puyallup tribe, these Indians would find they were left with only reserved land that was held in common by extended families in the Nisqually tribe. Under coercion and unclear negotiations, area tribes relinquished nearly all of Puget Sound and the Olympic Peninsula, some 2,240,000 acres, to the U.S. Government according to the terms of the Medicine Creek Treaty of 1854.

"Isaac Stevens saw treaty-making as a command-and-obey process, not a negotiation," writes author and University of Colorado law professor Charles Wilkinson. "Stevens knew what he wanted going in and did not plan on departing from his script." The two-page document was written in advance, in English, and presented to the Nisqually, the Squaxin, and the Puyallup tribes, who knew little English. Stevens then insisted the talks be conducted in the Chinook jargon, a mixed tongue of English, French and Indian words, used for trade. This jargon was a body of less than five hundred words. It was obvious to any learned observer that it could not possibly cover the issues of sovereignty, land ownership, fishing rights, assimilation, freedom, or any unforeseen issues.

During that time, Stevens asked one interpreter at the Medicine Creek site whether he thought he could get the Indians to sign the treaty. The governor was assured, "I can get these Indians to sign their own death warrant."

In his writings, Wilkinson questioned, "How could the Indians possibly know the transcendent meaning of what they were signing?"

Being ignorant of what was to come, Stevens had no qualms about Indian fishing. Fish and game were abundant to the point of seeming limitless. He could not fathom that in years to come hoards of whites would come to the beautiful area to overpopulate, pollute, and destroy the rights of others. But what did it matter or who cared? Stevens probably thought if anything was to become extinct, it would be the Indians themselves. "Essentially, the whites hoped we'd all die off," said Joe Waterhouse, a Jamestown S'Klallam Indian and a student of treaty history.

When the Medicine Creek Treaty was negotiated with the United States government in 1854, the Puyallup Reservation was formed, and the Indians were forced to live on 1,280 acres of land. They had to forfeit thousands of acres in what is now known as the Tacoma area: the Tide Flats, the township of Fife, and further north to what is now Federal Way. This included the area southeast of Tacoma where the city of Puyallup now stands. In return, the Indians were paid $32,000, something less than four cents per acre, to be issued over a twenty-year period. To make matters worse, in 1904, an Act of Congress greatly decreased the size of the Puyallup Reservation. It became the smallest reservation in the state of Washington at thirty-three acres of land.

Deprived of their original homeland, the small reservation became the only home the Indians had. On this land, the Puyallup found themselves virtu-ally prisoners of war. The Indians in the area soon experienced the restrictions of reservation life, as had other Indians further east. They found the dislike exhibited by the whites just as severe. They would remain in that state, for the most part, unable to better their way of life.

Stevens had no understanding of Indians and could care less about their ways and culture. But he could foresee the advantage of acquiring all of the land and its riches for the whites who were coming to settle the area. Luckily, the Puyallup and Nisqually stipulated, in article III of the treaty, that they must retain their fishing rights without making reference to reservation boundaries. History would later prove this would be a godsend to the Indians of the area "at all usual and accustomed grounds and stations."

As the number of whites grew, the Puyallup tribe found they were being herded into a smaller parcel of land, and their traditional fishing and migrating ways were being threatened. Since they were small in number, and not warlike, they were easily controlled by the whites who moved them, without conflict, from areas they had always cherished. In order to retain their fishing rights, the tribe had to forfeit nearly all of its land in the area.

Life became hard for the Indians. To help survive, they raised wheat, oats, and hay to feed what livestock they had. Survival was now the greatest challenge that everyone faced. The Nisqually were not accustomed to living in a new way. Now that the land was cleared of the forest, the large game was no longer seen. As a result, the Indians were forced to depend on their rivers, the Puyallup and the Nisqually, for nearly all of their food.

During the days of Tacoma's growth, the problem of exclusion increased. When competition for the salmon began on the water, bad feelings and forms of prejudice grew. In order to make it harder for Indians to survive, jobs were withheld and only seasonal agricultural work became available. When work ended in the nearby berry fields, the Indians had to travel to distant parts of eastern Washington, like Yakima and Toppenish, to find work in the hop fields and apple orchards.

During those difficult years, the Puyallup and the Nisqually struggled in a state of poverty. Their existence and rights became virtually invisible and ig-nored as the whites laid claim to everything in sight.

1. The Bay

COMMENCEMENT BAY has always been the center of interest for the people in the Tacoma area. Long before the foreigners came to lay claim to the water, the natives came to fish there and prepare their food supplies for the cold months ahead. They gathered to enjoy the potlatches and good tidings with other tribes with a winter festival of gift exchanges.

The salmon had always been the most important staple for the natives; their fishermen spent much time harvesting them and preparing them for immediate and future use.

A fall run of chinook salmon always occurred on the river along with coho, chum, and humpback. Steelhead, trout and sea-run cutthroat trout were also found there along with a threatened species of bull trout. Sockeye salmon were considered indigenous to the basin, but as time went on they began to decline. Neighboring tribes, the Muckleshoot and the Nisqually, also benefited from the great amounts of salmon that came annually into the Sound and directed themselves up the Duwamish and Nisqually rivers.

Native fishermen in dug-out canoes carved from Western Red Cedar were always ready to catch the salmon, in handmade nets, as they made their way up the river. After their nets were full of fish, they drifted into the Bay powered by the flow of the river. For the natives, it was the beginning of the season for obtaining food. At other times, Indians of other tribes, such as the Nisqually and the Duwamish further north, came by canoe to visit and enjoy potlatches and other festivities where the Puyallup River drained into the Bay. These gatherings would usually last days. At special times, when the sun was setting, blackfish came in pods, to the delight of many, showing only their dorsal fins as they searched for salmon and seal. For the natives, the large body of water was the common place where tribes gathered to fish, socialize, and carry out traditional ceremonies.

As years went by, the whites found that the water in the Bay was deep and could easily accommodate large ships. It was a natural harbor; in time, boats from many countries in the Far East brought goods from across the Pacific Ocean to establish trade. It was also the place where freight ships were loaded with domestic goods and produce, then shipped across the ocean to countries that lined the Pacific Rim.

Before the coming of the white man, the natives fished in their traditional way. They only took what was needed to get them through the year. During the salmon runs, the fish was caught at the mouth of the Puyallup River and the Bay itself. There was always fresh fish to eat, and much of the catch was dried for use until the runs of the following year. There was no need to overfish. Salmon was central to their diet and was supplemented by other sea life from the sound.

There was never any respect or consideration given to the needs of the natives. It wasn't long before the natives could see that their lives were controlled by all levels of the white community that was continuing to grow: the police, the fish and wildlife service, the press, the legislature, and the judicial system. Not long afterwards, the natives lost the freedom they had become accustomed to; they became stripped of everything dear to them with no means to challenge the rules forced upon them.

To enforce the new laws set forth, the Tacoma police patrolled the Bay and the mouth of the river nightly. They were always nearby to enforce their law against natives fishing. Their targets were always the native fishermen. At night, when most natives preferred to fish, the police were there to serve tickets when natives were found not using lights at the end of their nets or on designated places on the canoe. When natives did not have enough money to pay for the tickets, fishing gear and even the canoes they owned and used were confiscated.

The natives also had to be careful of tugs that would purposely direct their boats toward the outstretched nets to mangle them. Sometimes at

A traditional Indian canoe made of a cedar log used for driftnet fishing by the Puyallup and Nisqually tribes for centuries. Courtesy: © Bob Peterson.

night, whites would hide in bushes along the river and throw rocks at the natives as they floated by in their canoes towards the Bay. They proved easy targets once their driftnets were placed. Silhouetted by the lights of Pacific Avenue in Tacoma, they were easily seen. This behavior was commonplace during the 50s, 60s and 70s.

Most of the problems occurred on the Bay during the early part of the day when it was still dark. Numerous white fishermen harassed the native fishermen as they pulled in their nets. As time went on, they became braver and shouted obscenities at the natives as they went about their business of fishing. The natives maintained their composure, but it was difficult. They continued fishing and ignored the arrogant behavior of the whites. But the native fishermen continued to experience the ever-increasing harassment of the whites, which, at times, bordered very dangerously on violence.

21

As the natives continued to fish, they learned that it was dangerous to enter the Bay. They found it best to motor their canoes up the Puyallup River about a quarter of a mile, then direct their canoes downriver and lay their drift nets carefully in the water in a semi-circle. Once that was done, they would drift quietly and slowly with the current of the river to the mouth of the river; they were careful to lift their nets before entering Commencement Bay itself, where law enforcement authorities always waited.

Later, the number of white fishermen grew, and in time, they became a body of force and power that made it very difficult for the natives. The main purpose of the white fishermen was to control native fishing. Their goal was to restrict off-reservation salmon fishing by the natives and try everything under the sun to stop them from fishing in what they now considered their waters, the Bay itself.

Soon the natives found almost all whites in the area had formed negative opinions about them. The Tacoma News Tribune, the local newspaper, seldom printed anything favorable about native fishing. When it was learned that the numbers of salmon declined in Commencement Bay, the blame was placed on the natives. The whites claimed it was the fault of the natives because of their use of drift nets.

The natives observed that the press ignored the growth of hundreds of white fishermen in the Bay. The whole story was never printed. The natives knew when the salmon left the ocean, they entered Puget Sound and had to go through Commencement Bay before they got to the Puyallup River. The whites always got their first pick before the salmon ever reached the native fishing areas in the Puyallup River.

The natives knew that the trawlers out in the ocean took large numbers of salmon before they ever reached the Sound. They knew the amount of fish they caught was miniscule compared to the take of the trawlers. The natives knew the press ignored the foreign fishermen, basically the Japanese and the Russians, who fished the ocean. They knew these fisheries were taking great amounts of fish before they ever reached the inland bays. Since the U.S. government could not control them, the native fishermen became the scapegoat and were blamed for all decreasing fish runs.

The whites paid little attention to the harm that industry did to everything in the Bay and the rivers. They ignored the waste that was dumped into the Bay and rivers, causing much pollution. The natives knew this hurt the water quality by flow changes; this happened continually on the Tide Flats.

Logging operations up river caused soil erosion and de-vegetation along the stream banks. All of this affected the salmon spawning activities. The natives knew the salmon needed proper water flow and shade when they deposited their eggs. They wondered why the whites were ignorant of all this.

Now white people, in their quest for control, paid no attention to the fact that treaties signed over a hundred years ago, between the tribes and the U.S. government, authorized that the tribes were entitled to half of the catch within the boundaries agreed upon. They seemed oblivious to the fact that the tribes had given nearly all their land to retain those fishing rights. This loss of land proved to be a great disadvantage to the tribes in surviving everyday life and finally maintaining their culture.

A worse blow befell the tribes when the state legislature passed a Fisheries Code as a conservation measure. The Code gave the director of the States Fisheries Department broad authority to enforce its provisions, one of which flatly outlawed the use of set gear, a generic term that included the use of the kind of nets most favored by tribes. Thus, fishing on the Puyallup River, in violation of the Code, became a state offense, which in the view of Washington authorities could not be nullified by the 1854 Treaty, since the Puyallup River was no longer part of the Puyallup Reservation. The state enforced the Code simply on the grounds that conservation measures were necessary to save the fish.

The natives were beginning to understand that whites were untrustworthy and seemed to be above any law or legislation that did not favor them. If circumstances happened to bend in the favor of someone else, whites ignored it. Since they were now the dominant force in this country, they could interpret or rewrite history and laws so that it favored them. Their reporting would always be biased in favor of themselves. That is why the natives got unfair press. It was obvious that congress never consulted with the tribes when legislation that involved them was drawn up. The legislation was passed whether the tribes involved liked it or not.

The tribes were basically powerless against such odds. Their total number was probably less than three million throughout the entire United

States. They were exceedingly outnumbered not only in population, but also in wealth, influence, and consideration. The tribes would have to find another way to cope with the injustices designed by the white man. A level playing field to help the tribes improve their quality of life seemed very distant.

As the fishing seasons wore on, there were continuous confrontations between the whites and the native fisherman on the water. The natives became aware that every law-enforcement official in the state was against them, including the Fish and Wildlife Service, the State Game Department, the Pierce County Sheriffs' Department, and the Tacoma City Police. All were eager to arrest any native whom they deemed engaged in illegal fishing.

Now every Saturday on Commencement Bay, the white fishermen verbally abused the natives. Some ventured into the river itself to drive over the native's nets as they were drifting toward the Bay. At night, tugboats cruised the Bay and motored upriver looking for nets that were set. When they found them, they purposely rode over them and mangled them as best they could. Meanwhile, Tacoma police boats still patrolled the water looking for infractions in order to ticket the natives. It was obvious to the natives that the whites were trying to wear them down and break their will to fish. They knew now it was total war.

Early one morning, when it was still dark, a tugboat exploded as it was anchored in the docks of the Tide Flats. The natives were fishing nearby and were surprised at the force of the explosion. It shook everything, and the ensuing fire lit the sky. Within minutes, police cars and a fire truck arrived at the area with red lights flashing.

The natives recognized the tugboat as one that had motored over native nets nights earlier. They could see the extensive damage and were surprised that it was still afloat. They guessed it was dynamite that blew the boat apart. They wondered if anyone was killed. The whites suspected that the natives were responsible, but as time went on the truth was never found.

A few nights later, the native fishermen assembled in darkness at the mouth of the Puyallup River. The sparkling lights from Pacific Avenue in Tacoma could be clearly seen. They could see and hear the passing cars. The echoes of people talking could sometimes be heard if the wind was just right. Thoughts of their forebears came to them as the waves gently rocked their canoes. They knew that those who came before them had probably been there, in that exact spot, discussing important issues of their times. They wished those who had crossed over were there to counsel them on how to deal with the problems they were now facing.

As the fishing progressed, the whites continued to harass the native fishermen. The pressure increased as the days went on. From time to time, newspaper articles continued to indicate that the decrease of salmon was due to overfishing by the natives with nets. Most whites believed what was printed in the newspapers, and a growing number in Tacoma, who had never fished the Bay or had any conflict with the natives, also began to view them as the culprits.

Now the whites could see that the other natives who fished upriver in the Puyallup were becoming more apparent. In the past, they had always fished upriver and were never a problem. Now they were seen drifting their nets closer to the Bay. It was easy to see that the natives were instilled with a new confidence. One could observe it in the way they carried themselves. They had moved down river because they were unable to catch the fish they needed to survive. It also became obvious they wanted to be close if any real trouble started. They planned to support those who fished close to the mouth of the river. The whites could see that the natives were now less concerned with the power and presence they had exercised.

Weeks later a few native fishermen were confronted by a number of white fishermen on the Bay. One shouted, "When are you Indians going to get smart enough to know that you're stealing our fish? We all pay for permits to fish and you guys come out here without paying for anything, and take all the fish you want." He placed his hands on his hips and shouted even louder, "You guys are getting a free ride. You don't even do it in a fair way. You use nets. The poor salmon don't have a chance. You guys don't realize that eventually you will take all the fish, and there won't be any left for anybody. You Indians call us selfish. Maybe you should take a closer look at yourselves."

One native faced the sportsmen with determination. He looked directly at the one who spoke and replied forcefully, "It seems you had better study history a little more. None of you seem to know a damn thing about our issues that were agreed upon over a hundred years ago. We made those agreements and treaties with a government that represents all of you."

The native spokesman picked up his paddle and pointed it at the whites. "You seem to think that you brought the salmon with you when you came in your little boats across the big water. You didn't bring any riches with you. You found them here. Why don't you just hop back into your little boats and paddle on back to where you came from?"

The natives faced their enemy firm and determined. They were ready to make a fight of it. That day, close to a hundred white Sportsmen in their little motorboats surrounded the natives. No one moved. In the distance, at the mouth of the river, the whites could see the number of other natives, assembled in canoes, waiting and watching closely. They could also see a number assembled on the shoreline. This gave the whites added concern and they distanced themselves from the natives they were facing. Because of the number of whites gathered that day, most felt reasonably safe and confident but, still, they did not want to engage in any physical confrontation.

2. Satiacum

THE PUYALLUP TRIBE of nearly two thousand lived where the city of Tacoma now stands. The people were located on the Tide Flats and the Fife area and south across the Puyallup River to the small city of Puyallup. The forty-five-mile-long river flowed northwest and drained into what is now known as Commencement Bay.

Over time, the Puyallup culture developed, and was practiced and revered by all tribal members for centuries. Everyone could speak the language; they revered the stories told by the elders. Most were familiar with the songs and the dances that had been enjoyed by the people for as long as anyone could remember. These people were definitely fish Indians and they cherished their way of life.

The Muckleshoot tribe was to the northeast and the Nisqually to the south. The Duwamish were about thirty miles to the north. These tribes were just a close distance from each other and lived by a code that all understood and accepted. They were cooperative and enjoyed the friendly relationships that had been established and appreciated for centuries. The neighboring tribes that surrounded them followed a lifestyle that mirrored both the Puyallup and the Nisqually and all were friendly.

It was into this Puyallup tribe that Bob Satiacum was born in 1929. He first appeared in a little shack in the Fife area near Tacoma. Like others in the Puyallup tribe, his life began during an era of poverty and discrimination. The conditions arose before he was born, but grew because of continued white encroachment. Now that whites seemed to dominate the entire area, life became very hard for his family and the rest of his tribe. Satiacum and his family suffered like everyone else in the tribe. All Puyallup, he and his family included, depended on what salmon they caught in the Puyallup River to get them through each day.

Bob remembered what his parents had told him of the old days when they had more land. He remembered hearing that he was the great grandson of one of the Medicine Creek Treaty signers. Satiacum believed this agreement was made to insure his people the right to catch the salmon needed to survive. His tribe now found it difficult to live their lives squeezed onto a very small parcel of land. As time went on, it made him angry when he discovered how the whites had purposely denied his people jobs so they could not support their families. He knew why they were doing this. It was to break his people's will to live and grow in their own homeland. Satiacum was aware the whites hoped that his people would move, leaving what was left of their land to those who wanted more.

The only other thing that his people had left was the salmon in the Puyallup River. If they lost that, there would be no way for his people to survive. It was their only hope. He was aware that over a hundred years ago his tribe had given up almost all of their land to protect their fishing rights. He was beginning to realize that one day he would have no choice but to fight for the Puyallup fishing rights, regardless of the consequences.

All of these experiences had toughened him. He had learned early not to ask or expect any quarter from the whites. Bob understood that things would probably never change for his people. There were just too many whites in the area now. While still a teenager, he had only contempt for the white-skinned foreigners. In time, he began to accept the conflict with the whites as a game, not much different than that of cat and mouse.

The white culture had manipulated the Puyallup beyond any understanding or comprehension. Now, few in the tribe understood their culture in depth. Satiacum, as a young boy, could only remember parts of it, shared by his grandparents before they passed away. While they were alive, they taught him some of the words of the Puyallup language but even they knew only a small portion. Now, only a few of the elders were left who understood or could speak the language fluently. No one could remember, in depth, the songs, the dances, and the revered customs of his people.

The only thing Satiacum remembered vividly was how to fish and catch salmon. The men, and even the young boys, were still knowledgeable and expert at this. Before his father died, he shared his knowledge of the river and the ways of the salmon with young Bob. Once the generation of his parents was gone, the knowledge of most of the culture went with them.

Satiacum, like other young boys in the tribe, was affected in this era of hard times and prejudice. Most of his thoughts concentrated on the problems of his people. He was well aware that the whites had much and his people had little. He knew that the whites did not like his people and he understood that they had purposely made it difficult for his people to survive. Satiacum knew the methods the whites were using to control how his people lived. They thought if they could keep the Puyallup landless, with no means of making money to sustain themselves, these people would have to eventually leave and find somewhere else to live.

During his early years of fishing the Puyallup River, Satiacum saw number of white fishermen in their little motor-boats fishing with rod and reel on Commencement Bay. He observed their numbers as they increased every year. He could see that the numbers of salmon coming up the river were dwindling. This concerned him. Later, he became aware that the large ocean trawlers, owned and manned by white men, were the main cause of the shortage of fish. Their large purse seines could catch great numbers of fish in a single swoop.

As the years went by, Satiacum matured and could see the growing hostility of the whites toward the Puyallup fishermen while they were on the water. He could see that the bad feelings directed against his people were present everywhere: in restaurants, bars, stores, and even movie theaters.

When US involvement in World War II started with the bombing of Pearl Harbor, the Puyallup tribe was not directly affected by it. As the war progressed, rationing of goods appeared but this did not become a concern to Indians. They had been on rations for decades, far before the war began, and had become accustomed to it.

When great numbers of soldiers from Fort Lewis appeared in Tacoma for rest and recreation, Satiacum was surprised. For the first time he saw a number of Indians in uniform. Upon investigation, he found that many came from tribes throughout the country. He wondered how they were treated. Later, he saw that a large number of them had faced combat. He noticed that several had ranks equal to the rest of the white soldiers. They seemed content being in the service and were having no problems dealing with others. Later he observed the white soldiers from Fort Lewis held no animosity toward his people. In fact, they paid little attention to the Indians in general whether they were in the service or were only common citizens. They seemed intent on only having a good time, drinking heavily and finding girls with whom to share their time.

When the war ended in 1945, soldiers still came to Tacoma in great numbers. Satiacum could see that most of them had faced the enemy and proven themselves in combat; the medals they wore and the stripes on the arms of their jackets were numerous. While they were in Tacoma, the soldiers proved important to the overall economy. The Puyallup, for the first time, met whites who tolerated and did not look down upon them. This lasted into the mid-fifties when the armed forces were reduced in number at Fort Lewis.

When Satiacum reached high school age, he went to Lincoln High in Tacoma. Like other Puyallup who entered public schools, he had difficulty. There was no one to turn to when he needed help or counsel. His parents had little schooling and could not answer the questions he asked. Satiacum and other young Indians found that many of the white teachers cared little for them, and offered only limited help. Indian children sensed they were not welcome and many dropped out of school because of this. Those who remained in school had difficulty keeping up with their white classmates in the more difficult courses. Most did not because what confidence they had was further shattered by the attitudes and negative behavior of a number of white teachers.

Nevertheless, Satiacum was street smart. He was tough and competitive. He had learned at an early age how to survive, despite the prejudice directed toward his people. He did not believe, for an instant, that his people were inferior to the whites. He would not accept that the whites had a better way. Because of this treatment, he and others of the Puyallup withdrew into themselves and tried to ignore the ways of the white man. They adjusted and tried to live as their forefathers had. Measurement of any success within the tribe was never influenced by white standards, foreign to their ways.

In his early teens, Satiacum had grown to six feet in height and weighed close to two hundred pounds. He quickly excelled in the sports of football and basketball at Lincoln High School. He was very competitive in both sports. He was fast in the sprints, and a good shooter at baskets from any part of the floor. Satiacum was also a great defensive player on the basketball court. When he was on the football field, it was not unusual to see him running for touchdowns from all parts of the field. During his last three years, beginning in 1944, he was recognized as the foremost high school athlete in Tacoma. When this happened, he became respected in his tribe; everyone could see the strength and leadership qualities he possessed. Many could see that he might grow to be a leader of the tribe one day.

As he was growing, he would visit the taverns where Indians hung out on Pacific Avenue. It was in the taverns where Satiacum had learned to drink beer with other friends at the age of sixteen. If he needed recreation of another sort, he spent time talking with friends, playing cards or shooting pool. Early on, he realized that a number of good-looking girls came to the taverns; this made his visits there even more pleasurable. Flirting with girls, and spending time with them in secluded places in the evening, became his other great pleasure in life, besides fishing for salmon.

These taverns on Pacific Avenue were where Indians could congregate indoors. There were no other places for them to gather. It was in the taverns where they could meet others of their own kind. It was in the taverns where they could drink, play pool, relate to each other, and enjoy themselves without being looked down upon; they could let their guard down to escape the ridicule and prejudice that existed in the rest of the city. The taverns also became the places where the Puyallup could make friends and meet others from different tribes.

Soon Satiacum and others his age began going to the Old Mill. This building was once an old grange hall. It was located in the woods at the top of a hill, about a mile south of the town of Puyallup. Since it was turned into a dance hall it became a popular place for recreation for not only whites but also a small number of Indians. The whites and the Indians did not mix so-cially. There was never any communication between the two groups. Friendly

31

exchanges never happened. Drinking of alcohol was not allowed indoors and had to take place out in the parking lot. Sometimes, when too much alcohol was consumed, fights would break out between the whites and Indians. But for the most part each group stuck to themselves.

When late fall and winter arrived, the young were allowed to play basketball in the gymnasium at the Salishan School. Since a number of Indians attended school there, white authorities allowed this to happen. Soon teams of the various tribes that now lived in the area were formed and they competed with each other to the enjoyment of the Indian community. Bob loved basketball. He could be found in the gymnasium practicing in the late hours after the fish runs had ended.

One day Satiacum found an article in a magazine about a Mississippi Choctaw Indian. His name was Philip Martin. The article had a profound influence on Satiacum. He learned that Martin had served in the Air Force in Europe until the end of the war. Martin was impressed with how the Germans managed to put their lives back together after the war and were slowly coming back from the horrors of heavy bombing, starvation, and death. Martin could see that most of them did not have homes because of the destruction of the bombs by the United States and Britain during the war. Philip Martin was impressed by what he observed. He figured if the Germans had the will to bring back their economy and way of life, with planning and effort, his people in Mississippi could do the same thing.

Satiacum learned that the Choctaws had experienced much prejudice from the whites in Mississippi. Like his people, they were scorned wherever they went. When they could afford to go to the movies, they were allowed to sit in only certain parts of the theater, away from white people, next to the Negroes.

Satiacum smiled when he read Martin's quotation, "Members of my tribe were not allowed to eat in most restaurants in the area. That didn't bother us much. We had no money anyway." Bob could understand that type of poverty.

In time, Philip Martin set out on a mission for himself and his people. He believed in self-reliance and establishing an atmosphere of hope and prosperity among them. When he became the CEO of his tribe, he began establishing an array of profitable businesses and reinvesting millions of dollars into the reservation, dramatically reducing its dependence on the federal government.

Philip Martin was one of the great path-breakers in the movement of tribal self-determination. A news clipping stated, "What he's done is amazing, and it was grounded in the pursuit of self-governance. He was determined to do it his way, the Choctaw way, better than what the US Government could do." Because of Martin's efforts, not only natives were able to find employment but also Negroes and whites, as well. Because of his efforts the economy improved measurably.

Satiacum was impressed with the accomplishments of this man. He could see that his tribe faced the same problems. It would be worth the effort to emulate the Choctaw. Both were poor to begin with, but they still owned land. In addition, the Puyallup could still legally fish for salmon in the Puyallup River. Bob decided if he could earn enough money from fishing for salmon, that would be a start to go on to other things. It would take only wise thinking and determination. He felt he had both. He would use Philip Martin as his mentor and emulate some of his success. In time, Satiacum would apply himself to this goal. He had the confidence; he could make it work.

While fishing on the Puyallup River, Satiacum and his crew usually fished at night, after spending the early evening in the taverns on Pacific Avenue. Before heading for the river, they often had dinner at Harry Wong's Restaurant on Commerce Street. The place was easy to access and they were welcomed there. One had only to climb a long flight of stairs from Pacific Avenue to reach it. It was there, one evening, that he learned that Harry Wong referred to him as "Indian Bob." The name, created by the friendly Chinese proprietor with the twinkling eyes, amused Satiacum's friends and soon, when his brothers, Buddy and Junior, and then others wanted to needle him they called him by that name.

After the meal, everyone who smoked sat back and enjoyed their favorite brand of cigarettes. Buddy lit one and blew smoke into the air. "I like that name Harry gave you, brother, 'Indian Bob.' "Hell, it fits you like a 'T,' as whites say. I think I'll call you that from now on, Indian Bob!"

For years Satiacum had sensed that the salmon moved in greater numbers after the sun had set. He became aware that the Indians could avoid

33

harassment from the great numbers of white sportsmen during darkness. He recruited his brothers, Buddy and Junior, to help him. Satiacum and his crew established a pattern of fishing and became almost ghostly as they set their nets and drifted quietly in their canoes, powered only by the flow of the river. They would drift with their floats set in semi-circle until they came to the mouth of the river, as it entered Commencement Bay.

During their time on the water, the Indians never talked. They depended on hand signals to communicate. Plans were always made on shore to handle any emergency that might be encountered on the water. All were aware of the dangers of fishing at night and they depended on each other. They all knew that sooner or later they would encounter harassment from the Tacoma police, tugboat owners, or rowdy white sportsmen out to do harm.

After the salmon were caught, they were taken from the net and thrown into piles on the east shore near their cars. Each fisherman had his own pile, so when it came time to sell the fish to buyers, all could tell what was owed them. The salmon were left there until first light when white buyers of fish markets and restaurants came to bid on everything that was caught. The money they made enabled them to purchase other items necessary to live in the deprived world that all Indians had been forced into. The customers paid cash which allowed Satiacum to ignore any state sales tax.

When their catch of fish was sold, Satiacum and his crew would divide the money and then search for places to have breakfast. They learned that restaurants which would serve them were hard to find on the Tide Flats. They would have to drive further north in order to be served. The crew always left one man, with Satiacum's 12 gauge, to watch over their gear. After eating, they returned to where their canoes were docked and slept in their cars for most of the day. They wanted to be close to their canoes and equipment to prevent anyone from tampering with them.

During their off-hours, someone would eventually volunteer to purchase sandwiches, coffee in thermoses and other food for their late evening meal. They ate along the shoreline of the river, if the weather permitted. During rainy weather, they ate as they sat in their cars. When the sun was setting, they prepared again for another night of fishing. During the salmon runs, almost all of their time was spent on or near the river.

It was at these times that Satiacum shared stories about experiences he had when he was a young boy. "When my dad brought me down here I was very young. He taught me the ways of the river and the salmon. Everything I know of the salmon is what my dad taught me. I have fished every year since then. Whites didn't challenge us so much then. It wasn't until the early fifties, when the whites began trying to stop us from fishing. They'd tell us that all the salmon was theirs. That's when all the trouble began.

"Since then, our tribe was squeezed onto a smaller parcel of land. We were deprived of jobs in the Tacoma area. It became very difficult for Indians to make it from day to day. Soon, we became very poor and it hasn't changed to this day. Almost everything my tribe eats comes from the water. We hardly waste a thing. We can't afford to.

"It was different then and there were not a lot of buildings as there are now," Satiacum continued. "Tacoma was smaller.... less people... a lot quieter. Our tribe was smaller then and white people, for the most part, just ignored us. Later, when 'white sportsmen' realized they could have a lot of fun catching salmon out in the Bay, things started to change. Overnight, Indians presented a threat. Some of the white fishermen regarded us as a nuisance, and we became the target of their anger and frustration."

Satiacum raised his empty bottle to attract the attention of his waitress. "The salmon were large and they came in great numbers. The white fishermen always caught their limit and returned home, after a day of fishing, in good spirits. But later, the salmon runs began to noticeably decline. The whites became aware that the Indians were no longer using traditional homemade nets. They were no longer using spears. The nets they used now were manufactured nylon. They were longer and went deeper into the water. The Indians were beginning to use motors at the back ends of their canoes that enabled them to move quickly from one place to another. The whites feared in the long run the Indians would take more salmon, in fact too much salmon."

It was during this time that Satiacum learned that the dissension among the white Sportsmen was growing on Commencement Bay. They were not only grumbling about the new gear the Indians were using but they found out the Indians were selling some of the salmon to white buyers who came early in the morning each day. It angered them when they learned that the Indians were making profits by their sales. They did not know, or care, that the Indians needed to find a way to get money to purchase or trade for other food to take the place of the large game that was no long available to them.

From those days on, the animosity between the whites and Indians deepened. Decreases in the number of salmon were now blamed on the Indians. The whites ignored the fact that their numbers had increased. They were taking more salmon themselves, from the Bay, even before they reached the mouth of the river. They failed to recognize that ocean trawlers were taking an even greater number of salmon before they even reached the inland bays.

In their anger, the Sportsmen would sometimes drive their boats over the nets of the natives to damage them as they tried to dislodge the salmon. The aggression displayed never went beyond that, so the natives ignored the whites and continued to fish in their usual way. But as days went on, the natives could sense that problems on the water would grow worse and serious altercations would follow.

One night Satiacum observed that whites were hidden in the bushes along the river. He knew they were there to harass his crew by throwing rocks at them while they floated down the river with their nets adrift. He crept quietly to his canoe and pulled his 12-gauge from its case, took aim and fired it several times into the bushes. Satiacum's crew thoroughly enjoyed the sight of the whites scurrying about to get out of there.

When the salmon were not running and Satiacum needed spending money, he frequented taverns on the outskirts of Tacoma and Puyallup. A friend, known for his speed, always accompanied him. Satiacum had learned how to play the pinball machines and he had found a way to trip the mechanisms so he did not have to insert coins to play.

While his friend played the jukebox to distract the bartender and other customers, Satiacum would drill a small hole near the coin insert area and slip a wire to trip it. This allowed him to play without paying until the machine paid off. Before he left, he filled the hole with some chewing gum. This would hide the hole so he could use it again at another time. Satiacum usually made ten to fifteen dollars; that was enough to pay for beer and hamburgers for the night.

Satiacum and his friend always parked their car a few hundred feet from the tavern in case they were discovered. If they were, they sprinted to the car to make a quick getaway.

When the chinook season came, Satiacum and his crew worked closely and effectively together. They spent most of their time on and near the river. Bob regarded every salmon caught as a blow against the whites.

Because of the money he made and his free spending nature, he attracted women, a few of them white. He was never backward with women and now he made the most of it. At certain clubs in the Tacoma area, he could be found late at night drinking and having a good time. Indian Bob enjoyed this pastime immensely;it was not unusual for him to disappear for about a half hour or so with one of the girls that attracted him. After returning, he consumed a little more beer. Only his eyes revealed the merriment he was having. They seemed to warm and show a softer side of his personality.

Many of Satiacum's severest critics were racists. It angered them greatly when they would see him with attractive white women. When Satiacum would see his critics, he would graciously invite them over to his table and offer them a drink. He always found there were no takers. He would continue to fondle the women he was with and fill himself with the most expensive booze.

One night Satiacum and his crew met at the J&M Tavern. As they sat drinking, Buddy, Satiacum's younger brother, thought awhile and lit a cigarette. "In the old days the elders of our tribe told everyone that when this Governor Stevens came to talk to the Indians back in the 1800s, no one could understand him. He would say one thing, then the next minute he would say something else. Our elders, who understood a little English, had a hard time keeping up with him. No one could figure out what he was talking about or why the meeting was held in the first place. Our people learned that the governor was trying to get us to move from land that the whites wanted. He promised that the Great White Father in Washington D.C. would take care of the Puyallup after they gave up their land. The elders said that the saying 'white men spoke with forked tongues' came from that first meeting.

"Years later, our people learned how deceitful Governor Stevens was." Buddy continued. "We were once one of the richest tribes on this continent. We had much land and a lot of fish. We knew how to stockpile food for the future. It was easy for our people then. Now we are one of the poorest. But luckily our elders did not sign away our fishing rights. It's documented that we still have them. That's why we're still fighting for them on the water today."

37

Satiacum nodded at friends who entered. They seated themselves at a table facing him and ordered beer. With respect, they toasted Satiacum before they tipped their bottles. Satiacum nodded and explained. "The Indians have always considered Mother Earth a paradise. Whites don't consider it so. That's why they treat it the way they do. They hope the religion they believe in will help transport them to a better place once they pass away. They have done such a good job of making earth a hell for Indians that they actually believe Mother Earth itself might be hell. They are not smart enough to realize that this land could have been a paradise for everyone if treated differently."

While the three sat and drank, Satiacum continued, "A few days ago I drove up to south Seattle to see how the Muckleshoot were doing fishing in the Duwamish River. I brought my little motorboat along and went up the river into the Tukwila area. It was hard to believe how dirty the river was. It was obvious that Boeing and other corporations along the banks close to Seattle have been polluting for a long time, but I was surprised to see that people who live along the river are nearly as bad. When they want to get rid of something, no matter how big it is, they just dump it into the river. Entire cars could be seen deep in the river, completely rusted. It seems that all the whites that live along the river use it as a dump."

Satiacum paused as he tipped his bottle. "I saw a Muckleshoot with his net drifting. I asked how the fishing was. He told me that the runs were low. He didn't think the salmon that were in the river were healthy. When I dipped my hand into the water, it felt oily and smelled bad. Nothing could live long in that type of water and be healthy. One has to wonder what kinds of poisons Boeing and other corporations must have dumped in the water over the years. I question if it is safe to eat the salmon up there or anything else that comes from the water. When I was a kid, my dad took me up there and the river looked okay. Anyone can see that it isn't clean now.

"My grandfather told me that the Duwamish River was once beautiful. It wound, like a snake, north to drain into the Sound. There were trees and wildlife around the river and it was teaming with salmon, when they made their runs. During the late 1800s, the whites turned the river into a big ditch and lined the banks with concrete. They plowed over the natural curves of the river and straightened it. This destroyed the quiet, slow moving parts of the river where salmon like to spawn."

Satiacum's attention was distracted momentarily as a pretty girl passed by. Then he continued. "It looks like hell up there now. The whites have done nothing more than turn the river and the area near it into a huge garbage dump. All you can see now is decaying concrete and old dilapidated buildings. Almost all of the trees are gone and there are piles of junk left everywhere. No one seems to have any pride in the area."

Satiacum's friends listened quietly. One finally added, "It's surprising that the whites up there don't do something about it. After all, they live up there. It's right in their backyard. Some of them must be aware of what's happening."

Satiacum thought awhile and shook his head. "The problem is those whites that think are in the minority. The majority of them don't give a damn. The problem with whites is they live only in the present. They don't care about future generations. They have no care what their grandchildren will have to live through in the future. Their main thoughts are about making money now, no matter what it takes. They're willing to destroy everything around them to make a buck. Indians, on the other hand, have always had regard of those who will come later. Our people have always been considerate of others. Who in the hell would want to pollute the land and leave it in a mess for their grandchildren to inherit?"

A few weeks later, Satiacum went to the Duwamish river again, during the dark of night. He found a net fastened to the shoreline and noticed a small salmon. After retrieving it, he studied it. The fish was a coho and only a foot and a half long. It did not look healthy but he kept it and drove to Beacon Hill. He came to the house of a friend. They visited awhile and Satiacum left the salmon. Later, the salmon was baked and the family sat to have it for dinner but it could not be consumed because of the foul taste. One in the family said afterwards that the salmon smelled like diesel oil after it was cooked.

Not long after, Satiacum got into his canoe once again and went up the Puyallup River. He motored past Puyallup, toward Sumner. He could see that people who lived along the river treated it in the same manner as those who lived along the Duwamish. He could see trash and other discarded articles on the banks. Satiacum guessed it was there because those who lived nearby simply used the river as a means of discarding items no longer needed. He was somewhat relieved to see that the Puyallup River was cleaner than the Duwamish.

Satiacum was grateful that the salmon in the Puyallup still appeared healthy. He and his brothers had learned how to make big money in catching and selling salmon, but he wondered how long it would take before the river reached the condition of the Duwamish.

During the spring of the early sixties, Satiacum, his crew and other Puyallup fishermen began to experience more problems on the water. At times, whites who were merely spectators would drive down to the river and shout obscenities at the Indians. Satiacum could see that more whites were turning against them. Authorities were now arresting the Indian fishermen and fining them for what they called "illegal fishing."

This was making life more difficult for their families because they couldn't afford the fines that were occurring on a regular basis. It seemed as though they arrested Satiacum every chance they got.

It was the end of February in 1964 when Satiacum received an unexpected phone call. Marlon Brando, one of Hollywood's most famous celebrities, told him he would like to help the Indian fishermen in any way that he could. Satiacum was surprised and pleased that a world-famous personality like Brando would be willing to get involved.

Days later, the white citizens of Tacoma were surprised when Marlon Brando appeared. They could not believe what he stated in front of the press and the TV cameras. It was obvious that he sided with the Indian's cause. When questioned by the press, Brando made it clear that he was in Tacoma to support the Indians. He believed the Indians were right in their quest, their cause for adherence to the Medicine Creek Treaty, as it was agreed upon in the mid-1800s. Afterwards, Tacoma officials tried to dismiss his statements in defense of Indian fishing as nothing more than liberal propaganda.

Before he faced the press, Brando had been briefed about the problems the Indians were experiencing by Satiacum, Billy Frank Jr., a Nisqually from Frank's Landing, and Bernard Reyes, a friend from the Colville Reservation in eastern Washington. Brando proved more than sympathetic. He would do all he could to help the Indian cause while he was there. The Indians were impressed with Brando's attitude and his honesty. They could see that he was sincere and truly wanted to help them retain their rights to fish.

Trying to get interviews and photographs, the press
followed Marlon Brando everywhere during his visit
to Tacoma. Courtesy: © Bob Peterson

Large crowds, including TV stations and the press, appeared to cover everything Brando said and did. When the movie actor spoke passionately about the
Indians' right to fish, it was unsettling to the sportsmen. Some of them feared
that the words and stance of Brando would work against them in the long run.
They could see that many whites in Tacoma held him in high regard. Others
believed the press was going too far in giving him "good ink." The Tacoma
Police Force was somewhat confused in how they should handle Brando and
enforce the law.

On March 2, 1964, Brando walked the banks of the Puyallup with an Episcopal minister from San Francisco named John Yaryan. They boarded one of
Satiacum's fishing canoes and, along with Bob, moved out into the Bay. After
preparing their net and catching one fish, Brando removed the salmon from
the net. It was embarrassing for the whites when Brando stood and held the
salmon high for all to see.

As Brando helped the Indian fishermen place the salmon on the shore to be
sold later, the Tacoma police arrested him and Yaryan and drove them to a Tacoma
jail. They were soon released because no charges were filed against them.

The following day, Brando spoke in front of a full house at the Washington
State Capitol in Olympia. His manner was firm and his speech persuasive as he
presented his listeners with information about local tribes that they probably
had never thought about before. Many left that meetings more enlightened
than when they arrived.

Marlon Brando removing coho from a driftnet
after an "illegal" fish-in.Courtesy: © Bob Peterson

Now some whites in Tacoma could see some of the truth and wisdom in what Brando said. It made a number of them think about the Indian side of the story. Others began to understand the meaning of fair play and a level playing field that only their race had enjoyed during the last decades. Brando's appearance made a number of whites think a bit deeper about the conflict between the sportsmen and the Indian fishermen. Those whites who understood the law were beginning to see that the Indians had a strong case in their fight for the salmon.

While Brando was in the area, he visited Billy Frank Jr. and the Nisqually and was disappointed to hear what that small tribe had experienced while fighting for their fishing rights on their river. Later, he sent the Nisqually a check for $500.00 to be spent on anything needed by their people.

The Tacoma News Tribune had a field day while Brando was there.

The reporters were stumbling all over each other as they tried to get close to the actor to hear his comments. The photographers were just as bad as they snapped shots with their cameras every time the actor changed his posture. Brando received much attention from the crowds. Many could care less about his stance in favor of the Indians. It seemed that everyone had a sheet of paper or a magazine out hoping to get a signature from the famous celebrity.

Before Brando left the Tacoma area, he contributed thirty acres of land he owned in California to the Indians and apologized for being four hundred years late. Afterward, he was quoted in *Newsweek*, "Christ Almighty, in the name of justice, we have excised the Indian from the human race. We had over four hundred treaties with them and we have broken every damn one of them."

The appearance of Brando did not win the war against the white man on the water, but it did help. For the first time, the Indians got some honest press. His appearance gave a number of whites something to think about. He did not make any friends for Indians, but he did make some whites think about fair play and justice.

On March 2, 1964, Marlon Brando was arrested for "illegal" net fishing and taken to a Tacoma jail.
Courtesy: © Bob Peterson

Now, a number of whites in Tacoma began to express sympathy for the Indian's cause and some had a sense of appreciation for Indian culture. However, others dismissed it as nonsense belonging to a people of another time. Indian ways were foreign to the whites and many of them believed those ways would not work in a changed world. They were convinced that if the Indians did not change their ways and adjust to the present, they were destined to fail.

After Brando's visit, the battles on the water and attitudes toward Indians began to change. But it was clear the attitudes of some whites would never change.

Satiacum always had a strong interest in the welfare of other tribes around the state that depended on salmon as their principle food source. At this time, he purchased the largest Harley-Davidson motorcycle he could find. He wanted to travel south to the Columbia River to see how the Yakimas, the Wishrams, and Warm Springs were coping with laws regulating salmon fishing enforced by the state authorities. Once there, he found their salmon catches were small and nowhere near what they used to be before the Dalles Dam was completed in 1957.

Satiacum thought of how beautiful and powerful the river was before it was turned into a lake and no longer alive. He remembered how tragic it was for those tribes when they lost Celilo Falls and the huge migration of salmon that passed, heading for their spawning areas further upriver. He could see they were not doing well and having the same problems as his people.

As he stood on the shore of where the Celilo Falls used to be, his thoughts drifted back to earlier times. Satiacum remembered the friends he made, many of whom were no longer alive. As he studied the water, his friends seemed to appear before him, laughing and full of good spirits as they set their nets. He closed his eyes and thought of the old days. In his mind he agreed those were the best days, those times of the past when the water was pure and clear, when it was flowing powerfully and untold numbers of salmon passed upriver and when the tribes were happy.

Satiacum walked to a little park closer to the water and found wood benches placed there for tourists. As he sat there, he remembered the power and beauty of the falls. He thought of the powerful, churning river as it prepared to descend in thunderous cascades. In his mind, he could see the mighty salmon as they leaped to clear the surging water. He also remembered the fishermen of at least three tribes with their nets and spears; it was a wonderful time to witness. After minutes passed, he thought, no place in the world could equal the splendor of the Celilo Falls when it was alive and full of power.

Then he remembered his talks with his friend from Kettle Falls, further upriver, near the Colville reservation. He knew it was within thirty miles of the Canadian border on the Columbia River. Satiacum recalled visiting there when he was younger. He was awed by the power and thunderous noise as the river churned its way over huge rocks to fall at least forty to fifty feet below. He thought of the salmon, some over a hundred pounds in weight, who fought powerfully to clear the falls to go up river and spawn, to create a new life cycle.

Satiacum remembered when his friend told him the construction of the Grand Coulee Dam had destroyed the falls and the salmon that once came by the millions. It also covered the best grounds where camus, bitterroot and chokecherries were found. Satiacum felt a deep regret. He wondered if the tradeoff of huge monolithic concrete structures that generated power was more important to humans than the natural beautiful wonders created by the Great Power. Satiacum found it hard to accept that these great creations of nature, with the millions of salmon passing over them, would never be seen again.

The sun was setting and it was beginning to get dark. Before returning to Tacoma, he decided to have dinner at a restaurant in The Dalles. As he came to the entrance, he saw a sign on the door stating, "No Dogs or Indians Allowed." As Indian Bob studied the sign, he could see that the war over fish had reached beyond the shores of Commencement Bay.

3. Billy

THE NISQUALLY RESERVATION is east of Olympia, Washington, and situated near the Nisqually River. The land rests in the valley near the river delta and is north and adjacent to the Fort Lewis Military Reserve.

For centuries, the traditional territory of the Nisqually bands was the Nisqually River drainage. The forebears of the people ranged from the waters of Puget Sound (Whulge) to the woodlands of Mount Rainier (Tacobet). A legend states that precursors of the present-day Nisqually Tribe, the Squalli-absch, which means "people of the grass country," found their way north from the Great Basin and crossed the Cascade Mountains. They founded a settlement in a hollow presently called Skate Creek, outside the southern boundary of the Nisqually River watershed.

The Nisqually lived in peace for centuries with their neighboring tribes: the Puyallup, the Muckleshoot, and the Duwamish, further north. They were always on friendly terms with anyone who visited them. It was not unusual for the Nisqually to canoe to the mouth of the river and penetrate certain bays to reach Puyallup country, where they would stay for days visiting friends. Sometimes, they went further north to visit and exchange goodwill with other tribes such as the Duwamish, the Tulalip and the Swinomish. On longer trips, they visited the Lummi. Festivities were held for days as each tribe enjoyed the presence of the other. Since their cultures were similar, they had no problems relating to each other.

The Lushootseed language had been the traditional tongue of the Nisqually and neighboring tribes, and was a subgroup of the Salishan family of Native American languages.

In the 1800s, when the white people came to settle, life began to change for the Nisqually. At first, there were only a small number of whites and no problems resulted. Minor issues occurred later when whites built small settlements along the Nisqually River, but both the Indians and whites adjusted and learned to tolerate each other. As time went on, more whites came and began fishing the river in greater numbers. Soon the peaceful river became crowded when both whites and Indians gathered to compete for the fish.

Later, in the 1840s more land-hungry white settlers began to encroach upon the area. In the ensuing years, their numbers increased, which created tension between the cultures. However, the Nisqually remained peaceful and tolerated the presence of these foreigners. When the Western Washington tribes advocated war against the growing number of white settlers, the Nisqually leaders dismissed the notion and remained neutral.

For years the State of Washington regarded the Medicine Creek Treaty as an irrelevant nuisance. The State insisted that it could impose its fishing regulations on the tribes, regardless of the treaty. It tried to do so forcefully, destroying property of the Nisqually and making hundreds of arrests. But the traditions and training the Nisqually inherited were ingrained. The tribe had given ground and shed blood over the years but they were determined to fight for what was rightfully theirs.

Although the Nisqually had always been a peaceful people who would mind their own business, they would soon become the target of white aggression and domination. The problems worsened when territorial Governor Stevens, the single-minded charlatan, reinforced his motives for the sole purpose of taking most, if not all, of the Indians' land. White settlers could then move in and claim it for themselves, avoiding any payment that might be deemed fair. Centuries of Indians living on the land, treating it with respect, and creating a unique culture were totally ignored by Stevens.

The charismatic Nisqually leader, Leschi, and his brother, Quiemuth, refused to sign the treaty because of the meager provisions to Indians. While white settlers were being issued one hundred sixty acres of land per person, Steven's treaty gave each Indian only four acres on a small parcel of scrubland at a considerable distance from their life-giving river.

The original reservation was in rocky terrain and unacceptable to the Nisqually tribe, who were a riverside fishing people. This made it nearly impossible for the tribe to fish, their life-giving necessity. The Puget Sound Indian War, in which Nisqually warriors participated, erupted in 1855. The Indians fought courageously, but they soon ran out of ammunition and supplies and were heavily outnumbered. The Nisqually gave up the fight in 1856 when Quiemuth was apprehended by white soldiers and stabbed to death while under custody. Within weeks, the whites at Fort Steilacoom hung his brother, Leschi.

Many in the tribe came close to extinction. Smallpox, random violence and relocation devastated the tribe. Nisqually numbers fell from two thousand in 1800 to fewer than seven hundred by 1880.

Then in 1889, the first year of statehood, legislators closed six rivers to salmon fishing in the name of conservation. All were on Indian fishing grounds. The state eventually banned net fishing in all rivers, except the Columbia, effectively outlawing the Indians' main way of catching fish.

By the beginning of the twentieth century, the Nisqually, like other Puget Sound tribes, clung to the single-most-important thing they had left from their ancient culture: their relationship to the salmon of the rivers. The salmon fed them physically and spiritually; access to the rivers meant everything.

From then on survival was extremely difficult for the Nisqually. The people were restricted to their tiny reservation. They were deprived of outside resources and forced to fend for themselves. In 1917, the military confiscated 3,370 acres of their reservation to create the Fort Lewis Military Reserve. A number of tribal members were forced to cut themselves off from their cultural roots and seek homes elsewhere. This was the beginning of the dismantling of the tribe.

Billy Frank Jr. was born in 1931 near Frank's Landing on the Nisqually River where he spent his entire life. It was into this new way that he and other members of his tribe would be forced to endure and survive.

He learned to fish the river at a very young age, and when he approached his mid-teens, he was an accomplished fisherman. He was aware of every aspect of the river and the surrounding environment. Billy had been taught by his father, Willie Frank, and he understood the habits of salmon that came up the river to spawn. During those early days, the Nisqually were a healthy and handsome people, and they survived as they always had in intimate and close contact with the land, the Sound and the river.

The father of Billy was a great storyteller as was his father before him. Since the elders did not write, they kept the stories and culture alive by sharing adventures to others in the tribe late at night, after the work and fishing was done. Willie Frank lived a long and complete life for one hundred and four years.

In Charles Wilkinson's book Messages from Frank's Landing, the author quotes Billy. "I can picture Dad. He had mastered the art of fishing the Nisqually River when he was very young. He passed that knowledge on to me, as his father before him had shared it. This was how knowledge and traditions were kept alive within the tribe.

"Maybe he'd take fifty salmon. Then he'd go over to a gravel bar near the river, lay the fish down, and butcher them right there. His dad and granddad taught him everything about the fish." Billy added, "I knew how this worked because he taught me everything he and his granddad did, and my kids do it today."

At another time, Billy explained, "Then you take the fillets and weave three cedar sticks through them crossways. The stick up near the gill comes out on both sides so you can hang the fish on poles in the smokehouse. But you don't hang them up the first day. If you do, they'd drop off the sticks. So you let them drip and dry out a little, usually overnight.

"Dad would get his fire going in the smokehouse the next morning. He'd hang the fish on poles across the eaves of the smokehouse; the smoke comes out of the cracks. How long he'd leave them there would depend on what he wanted. You can smoke them just a little bit and get what white people call kippered. Or you can leave them in longer to cook more, smoke more. You can get jerky if you want, hard as a rock, and they'll never spoil or rot or mold. Later, you put them in water to soften."

Billy explained that his people had everything they needed when his dad was a boy. "Hunters in the tribe never failed to come back with furs and skins and meat when they went out to hunt. The Sound was close, only eight miles downriver. Dad would take a canoe down to the mud flats at low tide for clams, oysters and geoducks. He would smile and always say, 'When the tide goes out, our table is set.'"

As a young boy, Billy was taught to fish before problems reached serious levels of confrontation. On a cold December night, just before Christmas in 1945, when he was fourteen, he was arrested for the first time in what would become a long series of incarcerations for years to come. Two game wardens grabbed him as he was emptying his net of several chum salmon. He tried to escape but they caught him and held him by the arms, then shoved his face in the mud. Billy told them to leave him alone because he lived there and was only fishing to help feed his family.

Since then, Billy and other Nisqually fishermen faced continued confrontation from game wardens and members of the Fish and Wildlife service. Soon, they would face harassment from white sportsmen who claimed that Indians had no right to take salmon that legally belonged to white people.

This practice of harassment by whites was nothing new to the Nisqually fishermen. Billy's dad, Willie, was first arrested for illegal fishing in 1935 when Billy was barely four years old. From that time, the state began singling out Indian fishermen who were not getting state licenses or following state seasons or taking limits. In the late 1940s, the Nisqually River spring run of chinook, the biggest and best-tasting fish in the river, went into decline, falling victim to the unregulated offshore commercial boats and hydroelectric development. From that time on, white sportsmen laid the blame of declining fish runs on the Indian fishermen.

Billy was fully aware of all that was happening to his tribe. He had no choice but to discipline himself for a long fight. He knew his people were totally outnumbered but he had faith in those in his tribe who would fish and fight alongside him. He was aware his friends, the Puyallup, were having the same problems on their river and bay in the Tacoma area. He knew if his friends, to the north, were in deep trouble, he and members of his tribe would go to help them fight for their rights. Billy understood the Puyallup would do the same for his people if they were in trouble. Both tribes knew they were fighting the same war with the whites, a fight for the rights to fish, a fight for the salmon.

He fully understood that all tribes who had always depended on the salmon were fighting a war against an enemy who was greatly much stronger and had unlimited power. It was a war not only for a primary food source but a war that had to do with the maintenance of a culture, a religion and a way of life. Billy knew that the dominant culture did not and would never understand the Indians' respect for salmon. He understood that they would never comprehend their trust in nature. They would not appreciate how Indians measured their own existence by the health and well being of this important fish. He was sure they would never understand the strong relationship the salmon and the Indians had for each other.

Billy knew of what had happened to the tribes along the Columbia River who had lost their salmon because of the construction of dams. He knew of their poverty and the hard times they were now facing. Billy understood when the tribes lost the salmon, they were decimated of a power they needed to survive. He knew that salmon was the only body of wealth that the tribes had to sustain that power and well being.

Billy's education ended when he finished the ninth grade in a junior high school near Olympia, Washington. Later, he worked on a number of jobs that prepared the land for the construction of roads and ditches for sewer lines. To help pay the bills, he fished the river at night. At the age of twenty-one, he joined the Marines and learned about other parts of the world. This had been a dream of his since childhood. He learned how white people thought and what motivated them. Billy could see that the whites and his people had a totally different concept of life. He served for two years.

After his tour of duty, he returned home and continued fishing. Because of the increased pressure of the state's Fish and Wildlife authority, Billy and other fishermen in his tribe were forced to live and exist like outlaws, fishing at night, always on the lookout for men in uniforms.

The non-Indian salmon take rose sharply in the years after World War II. Forty-six Puget Sound commercial gill-netters fished for sockeye in 1945; the number increased to 322 in 1953, to 637 in 1957. There were 121 seiners in 1945, 452 in 1961. Salmon and steelhead were pursued avidly for recreation by new whites coming into the Northwest. Washington put a daily two-fish limit on sport fishing for salmon, but an annual commercial license, with no daily limit, cost $15.00. As a result, sport fishermen regularly purported to take up commercial fishing to get around this.

The intermittent harassment and sporadic arrests of Indian fishermen during this time escalated into a relentless law enforcement campaign of raids and stings. Regardless of the continued harassment by the Fish and Wildlife authorities and white sportsmen, the Nisqually continued to fish. They knew they were right and within the law of the treaty of 1854. The small tribe would disregard the ignorance and harsh treatment of the Washington State authorities in Olympia and proceed to fish the river as they always had. Because of the pressures the whites were directing toward the Indians, they suspected one day they would engage in a more violent way.

Overall, the Sportsmen hoped problems on the Bay would not reach a serious level of opposition. They had reasons to believe that if all-out war ever

With the exception of two years in the US Marine Corp., Billy Frank Jr. fought most of his young life for Indian fishing rights. Courtesy: Willy Frank

happened, the native fishermen would fight harder and present a greater problem simply because of their growing numbers. The whites suspected other tribes would come to help to make matters worse. Days later, what the sportsmen feared most occurred at another place and another time.

On October 13, 1965, at Frank's Landing on the Nisqually River, the most vicious battle between the white authorities and the Nisqually took place. One could see that agents from the Fish and Wildlife Services were supported by a number of the white Sportsmen; a small group of Nisqually fishermen were the target, many of them women and children.

Later when the Puyallup Indians heard about it, they were deeply concerned. After some of them viewed a film a bystander had taken, their anger bordered on rage. It showed, graphically, the violence that resulted in the bloody faces of their friends ~ adults and children ~ as they fought large numbers of whites who came to teach the Indians a lesson. One could predict there would be more trouble in the future.

When a number of Puyallup Indians understood the gravity of the encounter the Nisqually had faced, they were more than proud. All of them knew Billy and the Bridges family, Al and his wife, Maiselle, and their three daughters, Suzette, Allison, and Valerie. They knew those small number of Nisqually would never be intimidated by the large number of white authorities. The Puyallup respected them; they applauded the efforts of other Nisqually fishermen, including Dorien Sanchez and Buz Sawyer, who fought a hard but losing battle that day at Frank's Landing. They were especially proud of the small children who courageously fought to defend their parents by throwing rocks at the intruders who were using their nightsticks viciously. The Puyallup could see that the prejudice and harassment against Indians was reaching out to other areas beyond Tacoma and Commencement Bay.

When the Sportsmen learned of the incident at Frank's Landing they were somewhat surprised; others were pleased. They believed that the more support they got in their war against Indians, the better. After learning that the conflict was violent and blood flowed on each side, a number felt it had gone too far. Some felt it unnecessary when they learned that the agents also manhandled Indian women and children, beat them up and threw them in jail. But most felt that it was total war against the Indians, and everything that happened in war was fair.

After returning from the military to Frank's Landing, Billy eventually became known as the most important environmentalist and leader in the fight for Indian fishing rights.
Courtesy: Northwest Indian Fisheries Commission

After the battle at Frank's Landing, the Nisqually fishermen flew the American flag upside down at half-mast, as an international distress signal. It was a protest against the "broken" treaty promoted by the white Sportsmen and followed by the Fish and Wildlife authorities.

Before that bloody fight, Marlon Brando had come to speak up and support the Nisqually, a year earlier, as he had with the Puyallup. Brando made it clear that he believed the Indians were right in fighting for their fishing rights. He knew the case of the Indians was based on a treaty between the federal government and the Indians. He reminded the whites that a federal treaty was greater than any state law.

The hostile attitudes directed towards Indian people, by a large percentage of the public, was reflected by statements made by a judge and a prosecutor of the Washington courts.

Al and Maiselle Bridges, along with their three daughters, Suzette, Valerie, and Alison, joined Billy Frank Jr. in his battle for Indian fishing rights. Courtesy: Northwest Indian Fisheries Commission

Judge Jacques of the Pierce County Superior Court issued an injunction against the Nisqually, and told the Indians, "They never meant for you people to be free like everyone else."

Later, Pierce County Assistant Prosecutor Harmon in Justice Court said, "We had the power and force to exterminate these people from the face of the earth, instead of making treaties with them. Perhaps we should have. We certainly wouldn't be having all this trouble with them today."

One day Billy, in defiance of the pressures of white authorities, shouted, "This is our land. This is where we belong. We aren't going anywhere. We are here to stay."

This was his rallying cry to let the dominant culture know that the Nisqually and the neighboring tribes, who depended on salmon to survive, were determined not to assimilate in the American way but to live as their forefathers had for centuries.

Other pressures against Indians appeared when they were deprived of marketing the salmon they caught. When the state game wardens found buyers who would purchase fish from the Indians, their receipt books were checked. If the businesses would not comply, they were threatened with the suspension of licenses that would put them out of business.

As time went on, Billy could point to dozens of places along the river where Indian boats and nets were confiscated. He could relate stories of being chased and tear-gassed, and tackled, and punched and pushed face-first into the mud. He could tell of being handcuffed and dragged, soaking wet, to the county jail. This happened dozens of times to Billy and his fellow tribesmen.

Like his father before him, as Billy fished he was treated as an outlaw by Washington State authorities. He and tribal members, such as the Al Bridges family, fished at night and were always on the lookout for men in uniforms who wanted to enforce the law and manhandle them. Often, they were joined by friends ~ Don Matheson, Janet McCloud of the Tulalip Tribe, and others ~ who were dependable and always fought courageously alongside them.

Janet McCloud was a staunch advocate of Indian rights. When white authorities and sportsmen appeared, she was always present to help the Nisqually fight. She and her family had always fished alongside Billy and others of the Nisqually tribe. When harassed by white law enforcement officers, she would not back down in defending the rights of the Nisqually to fish.

To get a clearer picture of how Janet felt, she was once asked if she would vote in the coming presidential election. She answered, "Why should I? Presidents have never helped Indians. Besides that, I have never considered myself as American. Who in the hell would want to? I'm an Indian and will always be an Indian. That's good enough for me."

Janet McCloud was born in 1934. When she passed away with loving family members around her she had just turned sixty-nine years of age. Her Indian name was "Yet-Si-Blue," which means "the woman who talks." Everyone who met her had to agree that she did talk, always in defense of her people and indeed all Indians. When she entered the Spirit World in 2003, Indians and whites alike paid her the highest tribute.

When the salmon runs decreased in size, many whites in the Tacoma and Nisqually area blamed the Indians. The tribe, with Billy in the lead, countered and claimed the real culprits in the salmon's decline were commercial fishing, dam-building, and logging. In time, decades of research into the matter would prove that Billy and the Indians were right.

Eventually, it was found that the Indians only caught what was left over.

According to the state's own figures, Indians were catching less than five percent of the harvestable salmon in the region at the height of the fish wars. "Even to catch that, we had to go underground," Billy laughed. "To survive, to continue our culture, we had to become an underground society."

When finally brought to court, the only defense of the Nisqually was that they had the right to fish for salmon according to the century-old agreement between their tribe and the federal government, the Medicine Creek Treaty of 1854.

"Most of them didn't have lawyers," said Al Ziontz, a Seattle attorney who came to represent several Northwest tribes. "The Indians would cite the treaties, and the state would brush them aside, acting like the treaties were just pieces of paper that somebody found in a trunk."

It is interesting to note that those pieces of paper were never the Indian's idea in the first place. They were imposed, in no uncertain terms, by fair-skinned foreigners too powerful to fight. Eventually, the words on those pages would become the Indian's only weapon.

During the 1960s, the State of Washington increased their series of raids and stings. Much of it focused on the Nisqually River. Influenced by what was going on all over the country, by activists and civil rights movements, the Indians began to stage fish-ins in which the protesters openly fished in defiance of state laws. Billy was very much a part of these fish-ins. Many of them took place on his family's six-acre riverfront parcel known as Frank's Landing.

Today, a quarter-mile up the creek from the present day Frank's Landing, an isolated Douglas fir, now a dead snag, rises a hundred feet into the air. Interstate 5 lies only a short distance away. This is where the Medicine Creek Treaty was signed. Because of how the treaty was worded by the two-tongued Governor Stevens, many of the Nisqually tribe had difficulty understanding it. They soon realized that they would lose most of their land because of it.

Billy had worked all over western Washington trying to survive. He struggled with and overcame a drinking problem. He married and fathered children. He spent two years in the Marine Corps and saw enough of the world to know right from wrong. But with only a ninth-grade education, he didn't see himself arguing the fine points of law.

Billy had faced continued harassment from the whites on and along the Nisqually River since he was a teenager. After decades of affronts from

Janet McCloud was an important indigenous rights activist during the Fish Wars. Courtesy: Post-Intelligencer Collection, Ministry of History and Industry

Washington State authorities and white sportsmen, and after being arrested at least fifty times, he gradually began to rise to a respected prominence. During these long years, fighting for his tribe's rights, many who occupied seats in the State Capitol, in Olympia, had judged Billy Frank Jr. a dangerous child, a poacher, and a criminal.

Billy continued to fight for rights and justice. He spent a great amount of time in the courts trying to get an unresponsive State of Washington to live up to its responsibility of helping the salmon to survive. He was in demand for lectures all over the country. He spent much time trying to preserve and bring back a time that he once knew before the white man. When one listened to him, it was like listening to a humble advocate of the land and all that is a part of it. Through his words, he voiced simple truths indoctrinated by his father, Willie, and other elders in his tribe that only a few, today, can truly understand and appreciate.

Billy once said, "I wasn't a policy guy. I was a getting-arrested guy." He always ended his words with a laugh. Although he had faced the hatred of white authorities most of his life, on his own land, there was always humor. He never felt sorry for himself. He faced each day searching justice for himself, his people, and the salmon.

He often reminisced over that time toward the end of the conflict when the state responded to the fish-ins with a military-style campaign, using surveillance planes, high-powered boats, and radio communications. At times, game wardens resorted to tear gas and clubs, sometimes guns. To the disappointment and embarrassment of the state officials, these confrontations began to be telecast nationwide. People all over the country were now beginning to see the harsh methods of treatment the Washington State authorities and the white Sportsmen were using against the Indians. This had pleased Billy and many of the Indians in the Nisqually and Puyallup tribes as they searched for justice.

During those days of hard times Billy remembered one of his many talks with Bob Satiacum who stated, "The Indians are in a fish war with the whites, and many would get hurt along the way. It will take a long time to resolve it because the Puyallup fishermen will never give in to the demands of the whites. I know you, as a Nisqually, feel the same way. We know we are in the right because of the treaty with the federal government and no amount of harassment or jail time will stop us from taking our share of the salmon."

Billy recalled his thoughts of that day. He did not want a war with the whites. There were just too many of them made up of thousands of Sportsmen and those who supported them. On top of that, they were supported by the governor of Washington State, the legislature and the Fish and Wildlife Service. He was aware that both the Puyallup and the Nisqually were small in number and had no money or no support from anyone. Most of the time they didn't have enough money to hire legal help or get favorable press from the local newspapers.

Billy thought differences could have been avoided early on if both sides agreed to who was actually taking the most salmon and what was really hurting the fish runs.

The oft-arrested and jailed Billy Frank Jr., once branded a renegade for the civil disobedience he led, blazed a path to the cases that turned it all around. It would be hard to imagine in those early days that Billy would ultimately become one of the most respected people in the state of Washington.

After all is said and done, one would be hard put to find any person, in all of the United States, who has done more to protect the environment, its resources, the salmon, and the broader society. All of this was done under extremely difficult situations and over great lengths of time by one Nisqually Indian, Billy Frank Jr.

A clearer picture of this Nisqually leader can be seen and understood by observing his words. They represent the thoughts that had guided him throughout his life. Other Indians across this nation, who thought deeply, would have to agree and share these same feelings.

"I don't believe in magic. I believe in the sun and the stars, the water, the tides, the floods, the owls, the hawks flying, the river running, and the wind talking. They're measurements. They tell us how healthy things are. How healthy we are. Because they and we are the same. That's what I believe in."

4. The Quinault

In 1955, Taholah was a small quiet Indian village on the reservation of the Quinault Tribe. The community of about three hundred was located along the shores of the Pacific Ocean. Only a few white people traveled there because there were no roads that continued north. The Quinault Indian Nation consisted of the Quinault and the Queet tribes and descendants of five other coastal tribes: Quileute, Hoh, Chehalis, Chinook, and Cowlitz.

The boundaries of the Quinault Nation enclosed over 208,150 acres on the southwestern corner of the Olympic Peninsula; it included some of the most productive conifer forestlands in the United States. Today, there are great stands of western red cedar, western hemlock, Sitka spruce, Douglas fir, Pacific silver fir, and lodge-pole pine. Large numbers of Roosevelt elk, black bear, black tail deer, and cougar inhabit the dense forests.

The Quinault River still flows past Taholah, as it always has, then into the Pacific; for centuries there was little change. The beautiful river wound its way west through a heavy forest where the blueback salmon, a species of the sockeye, came to spawn. Many swore it to be the tastiest of all salmon.

This is where the quiet fisherman spent a number of years. His given name was Clifford Mowich but a number in the Tacoma area would one day come to know him as The Quinault. But one thing was certain; he was one of the best salmon fishermen anyone knew. This quiet man had a great sense of humor, and everyone had great respect for him.

Fishing for the blueback in the Quinault River provided him with the most pleasure and nearly all of his time was devoted to being out in the water in his small slender canoe. Sometimes, for his own enjoyment, he would row his canoe quietly for several miles up the river, stop and place his paddle inside the canoe. He would lie back and study the sky, then simply drift with the flow of the river back to the little community of Taholah. He had found this allowed him to think of many things that had always been a mystery to him. At other times he did this simply to admire the giant cedar, the quiet river and the beautiful scenery about him.

The boy loved this native area and he loved fishing in the Quinault River. His father taught him all there was to know about it, and he began fishing for the blueback at the early age of ten. He was always successful at catching the salmon, and from that time on, he was the one who caught what was needed to feed his family or others who were in need. When he wasn't fishing, he spent his time wind drying the salmon he caught for future use.

The Quinault was thirteen years old when World War II began in 1941, but because the tribe lived in an isolated area, the war had little effect on the community. Shortly after it started, the little community of Taholah observed armed soldiers passing through, marching north. They learned later that the troops wanted to make sure the shores of Washington State were protected from any surprise invasion from the Japanese.

The young boy's parents did not have a radio. Communication with the outside world rarely reached them. When The Quinault first heard of Germans and Japanese, it had almost no effect on him; he paid little attention to them. He did not know who they were or where they lived. He had heard they were the enemy, but this held little interest for him.

From their little community, there were a few of the young men who were called into the armed services. When they returned on leave, they shared more news of what was happening. But, by and large, the war and the fighting that took place seemed distant and far away.

In the mid-forties, when the Quinault was seventeen, he met Bob Satiacum for the first time. Satiacum, a Puyallup Indian, had journeyed

"The Quinault" (Clifford Mowich) traveled from his reservation on the coast to the city of Tacoma during the fishing season each year. Courtesy: Larry Workman, Quinault tribe

southwest of Tacoma to visit friends in the area. The two were close to the same age and became friends. The Quinault learned from that first meeting that Satiacum knew much of the Indian ways of fishing. The two teenagers had a number of things in common and they grew to respect each other. During that first meeting, while fishing on the Quinault River, they shared much of their knowledge of the water and the ways of the salmon and their people. Both enjoyed teaching and sharing their cultures with each other.

After The Quinault's stint in the marines and time in college, Satiacum invited him to come to Tacoma and fish in the Puyallup River for the chinook and the coho. The quiet man accepted the invitation and looked forward to making the trip. He thought fishing in another river would be interesting. He loaded his canoe and Evinrude motor on a rack, and then packed his rain-gear, rubber hip boots, and extra clothing. His trusty 1940 Chevy pick-up was ready for the trip.

The Quinault had grown to be a slender man, five feet ten inches tall. He was a quiet man with a chiseled face and aquiline cut nose. His dark observant eyes, defined by sharp curved eyebrows, appeared to be always alert. Tight thin lips showed little emotion. When he moved, it was effortless.

His fingers were long and thin, almost delicate, but they were strong, as if made of steel.

When The Quinault arrived at Satiacum's place, the Puyallup was pleased to see him and looked forward to showing him the big city of Tacoma. After unloading The Quinault's pick-up and showing him the room where he would spend the night, Satiacum drove him to the mouth of the Puyallup River where he pointed out Commencement Bay and explained that the white sportsmen fished there; it was considered off limits to his people. Later, Satiacum drove to Pacific Avenue and showed The Quinault the Indian taverns where his people spent their leisure time. He added this was the only place in town where Indians were welcome.

Bob drove the length of Pacific Avenue, showing off three movie theaters along the way, then down Commerce Street where inexpensive lodging could be found. Commerce Street was close to the center of all activities in town and near the river where they would fish.

The Quinault was impressed with everything he saw and knew he would enjoy spending the fishing season in this new location. The Quinault remembered, from his earlier years, that Tacoma had a large number of people and cars that seemed to be everywhere. On the Quinault Reservation in the little town of Taholah there were only tribal members and a few cars. He was greatly surprised at the number of soldiers that walked the streets. They all seemed to be in a good mood and having a lot of fun. The Quinault could see that most had faced combat by the ribbons and medals displayed on their uniforms.

As Satiacum drove him back to his house, The Quinault could not wait to start fishing and making money so he could take in a movie at one of the theaters in town. He thought he would also like going to some of the taverns he saw to have a beer and meet some of the Indians that spent their time there.

That night Satiacum drove his friend to where his brothers, Buddy and Junior, lived. He wanted to introduce them to their new fishing partner from the Quinault Reservation. Satiacum was pleased The Quinault agreed to join them. He was well aware that The Quinault was a great fisherman. He was sure they would work well as a team fishing for the salmon at the mouth of the river.

The next day, The Quinault found a small apartment to his liking. There was a sofa that could be made into a bed and a small kitchenette where he could cook, if he felt like it. The apartment was small and inexpensive. He was pleased with the location because he could see Pacific Avenue below and all the activity that took place there.

After he was settled in, he walked the streets of Commerce, Pacific Avenue, and Broadway. He enjoyed studying the many stores. He was again impressed with the number of white people he passed. The Quinault had never seen so many. As he was returning to his apartment, he found Harry Wong's Restaurant. He remembered Satiacum telling him that it was a good place to eat; he decided to give it a try. The Quinault was pleased to see the prices were reasonable.

After some trouble ordering, a waitress who appeared to be Indian, walked over to help him. She introduced herself as Mary. After ordering, he asked her what tribe she belonged, and she responded, "A Lakes Indian from the Colville Reservation. I was born on Red Mountain in British Columbia near a small town called Rossland."

The Quinault was interested because he had never been east of the mountains, much less Canada. He had heard of Colville Indians but he had never met one.

After Mary returned from the kitchen with his serving, he began eating. He was immediately fascinated by the flavor of the food. He had never experienced such tastes. As he ate, he found he could not recognize some of the ingredients in the dishes before him. But the food was good and he soon finished his meal.

Mary came over and placed a small plate of what appeared to be some sort of pastry on the table. The Quinault, somewhat unsure of himself, bit into one and found a message inside. This surprised him; he had never seen anything like it before. He sat and read the printed matter.

Business was slow so Mary sat down in the booth across from The Quinault. "Those are fortune cookies," she informed him. "You can have your fortune told here after dinner each evening for free. She smiled and continued speaking. "My parents weren't actually living on Red Mountain when I was born; they were there for the huckleberry season. It was an annual trip for them; only a forty minute drive from our home in Castlegar."

"What brought you to the U.S.?" the Quinault asked.

"Well, after my mother died when I was six, a religious group from Russia came in large numbers to take our land, crowd us out, you might say. The only way we could get to our house was to cross the Columbia river and row up the Kootenay by boat. These foreigners were so land hungry they even pushed over the gravestones of my family." Mary paused a moment to light a cigarette. "My father's name was White Grizzly Bear. He tried to get the provincial government in Canada to help but they just ignored him. My father and I soon left Castlegar and travelled south, crossed the border and settled at Kettle Falls on the Colville reservation."

The Quinault thought wryly of those who were strongly religious but had no trouble in breaking commandments when it came to serving their personal needs. "It would seem the provincial government in Canada is as useless and devious as the government in the United States." He stated with conviction.

Over the next few months, Mary taught the Quinault everything he needed to know about the mysteries of a Chinese menu. He learned to associate what was printed on the menu with dishes he liked. The Quinault found she was helpful and outgoing and very attractive.

The Quinault was pleased with his first Chinese meal. He sat back and lit a cigarette. A small Chinese man walked over smiling and introduced himself as Harry Wong. The man was short, about five feet two inches tall. He looked friendly and accommodating. The Quinault found that every time Harry smiled his eyes twinkled. He grew to like Harry immediately. While the two talked, the number one cook came from the kitchen. He was a big man in his mid-sixties. Harry introduced him as Chester Wong. The Quinault noticed that Chester held a cigarette tightly crimped in the middle of his mouth. He appeared to be frowning; but in reality he was usually deep in thought.

The following Friday night was The Quinault's first time fishing in the Puyallup River. He had already prepared his canoe by loading his drift-net and paddle. He placed a large thermos of hot coffee under the seat where he would sit. He tied a kerosene lamp to an inner-tube and attached it to the end of his net. He talked momentarily with Satiacum and his brothers and then put on a life jacket and climbed into his canoe. He started the motor of his Evinrude and followed the crew up the river. After motoring for a

Chester Wong, the chef at Harry Wong's restaurant,
befriended "The Quinault" while he lived and fished
in Tacoma. Courtesy: Teresa Wong

quarter mile, they all set their nets in a semi-circle and floated quietly to the mouth of the river powered only by the drift of the river.

After his first night of fishing on the Puyallup with Satiacum and his crew, The Quinault decided to drive down to the mouth of the Puyallup later and watch the activity on Commencement Bay. It was Saturday morning and the sun was out. It promised to be a fine day. When he arrived he was taken aback by the large number of whites who were already out on the water. He could hear the revving of motor boats and the loud talking and shouting before he got there.

He remembered when Satiacum told him they would be fishing close to white Sportsmen who did not hold Indians in high regard; it piqued The Quinault's curiosity. Up until the day before, he never paid much attention to whites. He had seen whites when he was in the service and during his time in college but never in a fishing boat. As he stood on the shore, he was surprised, then perturbed, at the noise made by the motorboats and the shouting of the white fishermen. It was never-ending and very disturbing. He decided to spend the rest of the morning elsewhere, someplace quiet.

A few days later, more observation of whites left him somewhat confused. He was interested to see that all of the whites were not alike.

The many soldiers that crowded the streets were from Fort Lewis. They seemed friendly and were there for seemingly one purpose only, to have fun. Out on the water of Commencement Bay, the whites who fished were different. They were more serious and seemed to harbor thoughts of complete possession. They seemed to think that they owned the Bay and all the life that was in it. The Quinault could see that the whites felt they had the right to exclude everyone they didn't like from fishing there.

At night when the crew fished, he was surprised to see that those who operated the tugboats and, even the Tacoma City Police, reinforced the white Sportsmen. When, by chance, the Indians entered Commencement Bay, they were quickly harassed by the authorities and sometimes jailed if their nets were set or if they possessed any salmon in their canoe. The Quinault could see that his friend, Satiacum, and the people who fished with him were in the midst of a strong force. He was aware they were greatly outnumbered. The Quinault could see that serious problems could erupt at any time.

On weekends, when the whites were on Commencement Bay, something seemed wrong. They were loud and boisterous as they spoke and consumed large amounts of beer and whiskey. When they revved the motors of their boats and went from one place to another, searching for better places to fish, it was disturbing. To The Quinault the noise they made was foreign to the area. The white Sportsmen, laughing and yanking salmon in with their bright shining poles, seemed almost irreligious.

One day, while studying himself in front of the bathroom mirror, he noticed he needed a haircut. He remembered seeing a barber shop on Commerce Street and decided to stop by it on his way to an early matinee. He learned it was a school that taught people to become barbers. The Quinault noticed that the prices were low. As he sat waiting for the next free barber, he picked up a magazine and began reading. He came upon an article entitled The Ten Commandments. This interested him. After reading it thoroughly he thought about it and agreed that the concepts in the commandments were similar to what he was taught by elders in his tribe. He was pleased to see them in printed form. The words were powerful and meaningful to him. He knew he had always patterned his life as the words were written. He felt good simply by reading them. The

Quinault believed if everyone patterned their lives as the words were written, the world would be a better place.

As he stood on the shore of Commencement Bay, he again studied the activity of the whites on the water. The Quinault could see that the whites were not following what the commandments had intended to impart. He could count at least three of the commandments the whites had already broken before it was time for lunch. He assumed most went to church every Sunday to pledge allegiance to their commandments, only to break them during the remaining days of the week. Then, on the following Sunday morning, they would congregate solemnly in their churches, on their knees, to swear their allegiance once again.

The more The Quinault observed the whites, the more interesting they became to him. One day he studied them from a distance in his slender canoe, rocking gently with the waves. As the rain fell heavier, he pulled the hood of his raincoat over his head, hunched his shoulders and munched on a strip of smoked blueback. It was obvious that the behavior of whites fascinated him.

Since coming to Tacoma, The Quinault had developed a pattern of living that suited him. Before going out to the river at night for fishing, he would sometimes spend the earlier part of the evening at Harry Wong's Restaurant. The Quinault liked the place. Sometimes, when business was slow, he and Chester sat across from each other in a booth, sharing cigarettes and talking about a variety of things. At first, The Quinault had difficulty understanding Chester because of his broken English. Gradually, he adjusted, and the two shared many of their feelings about life and what was happening about them.

It was during this time that The Quinault remembered the great size of China and its people. He had always thought that America was large. He was beginning to understand there were many white people across this country, maybe too many, but he learned that in no way could it compare to the masses in China. He remembered his time as a Marine. During his days of service, he was a pilot who flew cargo to northern China. Those were interesting days. He was always occupied. He recalled he never had a chance to meet the people of China. He was too busy flying supplies to remote places further north.

One evening, to the delight of Harry and Chester, The Quinault came in from the river with a fifteen-pound coho. It was a beautiful fish. There was a storm brewing, the wind was blowing, lightning was flashing, and it was raining heavily. Because of this, The Quinault decided to take the night off. Chester quickly took the fish into the kitchen, cleaned it and stored it in the refrigerator for future use. He returned, with two cups of coffee, and invited the man from Taholah to sit with him and warm up. That was the night that The Quinault learned something about China he had never heard before.

"You know man called Columbus" Chester asked. "Say he discover America."

The Quinault quickly challenged this claim, "How could anyway lay claim to a place occupied for centuries by others?"

Chester exhaled a thin line of smoke and smiled broadly. "China come here to this America maybe over seventy years before that man Columbus. Come in big ships, maybe three hundred feet long, maybe thirty thousand men in fleet. China not come to conquer or steal. China come to learn. Hope to make trade one day."

The Quinault found this information very interesting and to his liking. He recalled how the tribes had been treated by the white fishermen and all of the white authorities. He remembered how whites, who owned businesses in the city of Tacoma, refused to give Indians jobs when they needed them most. The Quinault agreed the Indians would have been better off if the Chinese had stayed and shared their humanity and knowledge after landing on these shores. There were times before fishing when The Quinault found Chester playing pool at the J&M late in the afternoon, during his off hours. He was impressed to see him dressed in a fine sportscoat, matching slacks and brown polished dress shoes. Chester seemed to be a different man. The attire was different from Chester's accustomed dress as a cook: a white shirt, matching pants, an apron, white sneakers, and a white chef's cap. Only the crimped cigarette in the middle of his mouth remained the same. Since The Quinault enjoyed pool himself, he would play Chester at ten cents a game. They would play until it started to get dark, when it was time to return to the river to fish for the night. As months passed, the two became good friends.

The Quinault soon learned that going to the matinees at one of the theaters on Broadway or Pacific Avenue was a good way to spend afternoons. Now he had a chance to appreciate a variety of movies that had never been available to him before. He was content to sit and watch the movies by himself, close to the screen munching on a sack of popcorn, just as the white kids did. When he saw a movie starring Marlon Brando, he was impressed. He felt he was the best, by far, at this profession of make believe.

On those evenings when he was not fishing, The Quinault enjoyed sitting in one of the taverns on Pacific Avenue, quietly smoking and enjoying a beer. For the sake of variety, he always chose a different tavern. He never sat in the same tavern two nights in a row. There were times when a very attractive young lady would come into the taverns. After studying her, he agreed she was the most beautiful woman he had ever seen. The Quinault later learned she was a Nez Perce and her name was Zola Kipp. He noticed she had many friends who would buy her drinks late into the night.

But The Quinault cherished solitude and always sat by himself. This allowed him to concentrate on the problems between the whites and the Indians. When The Quinault thought of his adventures out in the river and the Bay he found there was a difference between the white Sportsmen and the Indians reasons for fishing. For the whites, it was merely a sport, whereas with the Indians it was a matter of survival. He remembered the age-old trust between the Indians and the salmon. He had always believed that both understood their role and why they were there. The Quinault accepted that both knew their purpose in the overall scheme of life.

The Indians took only what was needed to feed their families and themselves. When they took the salmon from the nets, they always asked forgiveness and thanked the salmon for the food they would provide. The salmon seemed to accept this. Most of the salmon were allowed to go upriver to spawn and prepare for another life that they were a part of. This had always been the accepted practice for as long as The Quinault could remember. It was a natural procedure for both the Indian and the salmon that worked. They seemed to complement each other. There was always a balance that all understood and followed naturally. On the other hand, the whites seemed to fish only for the fun of it. They never seemed to show respect to the salmon that would eventually be a part of them.

During the salmon runs each night, Indian fishing mirrored the preceding night for The Quinault. He was satisfied with his life in Tacoma. He had made some good friends in the Puyallup tribe and others who frequented the taverns. But the large Chinese man was always his favorite acquaintance. He treasured his time with Chester.

In time, The Quinault learned to accept the presence of hundreds of white Sportsmen on Commencement Bay. He eventually grew to expect the confrontations that occurred when they were around. However, their angry assaults on the Indians failed to disrupt his pattern of fishing. When surrounded by them and hearing their condemnations of Indian fishing, he went about his business of quietly netting fish and ignoring their presence. When the whites lost control of their emotions and verbally assaulted the Indian fishermen on Commencement Bay, the Quinault ignored them and simply proceeded to catch more fish.

As always, The Quinault caught the most fish in the river. He knew instinctively the patterns of the salmon. This knowledge was in his blood. Members of the Puyallup and Nisqually Tribes had this instinct, also, but his knowledge was deep within him and he showed it when fishing on the river. This ability came to him when he was very young, when he first fished the Quinault river. Everyone had to admit, when the chips were down, the quiet, slender fisherman from Taholah could not be matched.

The Quinault found his months fishing in Tacoma rewarding. He remembered the area called the Narrows where he was born and first went to school. During those years he was never impressed with the area. He was pleased that his family decided to move and live in a quieter place, where there was much solitude.

While in the taverns on Pacific Avenue, he had met Indians from different parts of the country: the plateau and the plains. At other times, he met those of the coastal tribes, such as the Duwamish, Muckleshoot, and the Nisqually. He particularly enjoyed listening to those who could speak their language. He felt that the Sioux tongue was very beautiful when someone who was fluent spoke it. He was always amazed at how different the languages were among the tribes.

As he sat in the J&M he thought of the many experiences he had in Tacoma during the season. Fishing in the Puyallup River enabled him to make enough money to live on until the following spring. Although he missed the beauty and quiet atmosphere of Taholah, he figured he could put up with the noise and fast-paced activity of Tacoma. With some effort he could tolerate the behavior of the white Sportsmen during the fishing season. He could do this until the salmon runs ended in late October and then he could return home. When that time came The Quinault told Satiacum he would return in the spring, when the new season began. Satiacum nodded and helped load his canoe on the rack of his pick-up. He walked over to retrieve The Quinault's belongings and threw them into the back end of the pick-up.

Afterwards, as they stood by the shoreline looking out at the water, they watched Buddy and Junior quietly drifting with the current in their canoes. Their floats and nets were laid in the familiar semi-circle. To The Quinault, this was always a fine thing to see. The two waved good-bye as they floated by. Although they were experienced fishermen, they learned much about the character and habits of salmon from this man from Taholah.

Before getting into his pickup, he shook Satiacum's hand and told him he would see him next season. As he traveled south, he wondered if the tension between the Indians and the whites in Tacoma would ever let up. He thought about the rules invented by crafty whites to control others; rules that always seemed to benefit the whites. If the whites found that those who the rules were designed to control could not be dealt with, they usually found ways to turn the rules into laws. He remembered at one time there was a law that prevented Indians from hiring an attorney to defend themselves when they needed help. This angered The Quinault whenever he thought about it. He agreed that the plight of Indians had not changed much over the years. What made it worse is that all who enforced the laws, those who sat on the bench in the courts and passed judgments on the laws were white. He shook his head in wonder at how all this came to be.

As he continued his trip home, the rain started to fall and he turned on his windshield wipers. He checked through the rear-view mirror to see how his canoe was riding on the rack behind him. The Quinault decided to concentrate on simpler issues like driving his old, worn Chevy pick-up and admiring the scenery. He shifted into second gear and slowed as he approached Olympia. As he passed the state's capitol, he directed his thoughts to returning home. He had missed Taholah, where it was always quiet. He missed fishing for the wonderful blueback in the beautiful, pristine Quinault river. He could not wait to catch one and cook it next to an open fire that burned alder. He would add only a sprinkle of salt when the fish was cooked. He was sure they were the best tasting sockeye in the world.

Where he lived in Taholah, there were no protests against Indian fishing. He knew the whites had not yet discovered the wonderful blueback in the Quinault River. He mused as he thought about the future and what might happen if whites finally found his beloved river. He hoped it would never happen.

5. Bernard

IN 1955, after graduating from Okanogan High School in a little town in eastern Washington, Bernard Reyes took a greyhound bus to Tacoma to visit his mother. He hoped he would be able to find a job. He had tired of thinning apples in the local orchards during the last four summers and wanted to try something new. He had been to the city on the coast before with his older brother, Lawney. They had hitchhiked there in the summer of 1951. Earlier that same year his sister, Luana, had moved to Tacoma to live with their mother after graduating from high school.

He found that living in a city was indeed unlike the little town of Okanogan. At that time, he thought Tacoma was the biggest city in the world. Bernard spent many hours walking the streets and window-shopping. He was impressed with uptown Tacoma, especially Broadway. He was awed by all the movie theaters within blocks of each other, at least five of them in all. He wondered about the expensive merchandise that was on display in most of the windows of the stores in the area. He reasoned that only the rich could afford such things. The only people in this part of Tacoma were whites. Bernard was greatly impressed with the beauty of the large houses they lived in. He was amazed that they could afford to live there.

At times his sister, Luana, accompanied him and introduced him to the streets and places of business that she thought might interest him. She showed him the upscale restaurants, occupied by white people, which were found only at upper Broadway and St. Helens. At other times, as they

Bernard's sister, Luana, introduced him to the city
of Tacoma. He was amazed at the number of white
Sportsmen fishing in the Bay. Courtesy: Teresa Wong

walked, she showed him the Puyallup river and Commencement Bay; this
large body of salt water that bordered the city and what sea-life that was seen
fascinated Bernard.

Sometimes, the two would watch Indian fishermen securing their nets
near the banks of the river. When the Indians were in their canoes Bernard
found it interesting as he observed them setting their nets in a half circle to
drift slowly with the tide. Now and then, he saw the cork floats holding the
net sag, then disappear in the water. He learned later that salmon pulled
the floats under when they hit the net. At other times, they watched others
in their slender canoes carved from cedar logs floating quietly down to the
mouth where the river drained into the Bay.

Bernard enjoyed his walks around Tacoma with his sister. He had always
regarded her as intelligent and totally unselfish. She had taught him almost
everything he knew.

Besides the Indians fishing, he found the Bay itself fascinating with
all types of sea-life that he had never seen before. They walked along the
shoreline itself and studied clams, starfish, and other life from the water.
When they studied the water carefully they could see jelly-fish floating
quietly near the surface.

It was during these times that he discovered the smell of the area along
the river was very different than Broadway and the northern parts of the

city. He wondered what made the smell of this part of Tacoma so noxious. He recalled that his mother lived on the Portland Avenue area, near several other Indian families, and they suffered the most from this distasteful smell. Bernard thought this surely couldn't be healthy. He learned from Luana that the smell came from the exhaust fumes of the St. Regis Mill located further north on Commencement Bay. At the end of their day, he and Luana would enjoy dinner at the Chinese restaurant that their mother Mary and Harry Wong ran on Commerce Street.

One day, Bernard discovered a number of Indians who lived close to his mother in the Portland Avenue area. He learned from her they were members of the Puyallup Tribe. This was the first time he had ever met Indians other than those of his own, the Colvilles. Bernard noticed the similarities between the Colville and the Puyallup but there were also differences. They seemed to be reticent and shy. The Puyallup pronounced words in a different manner than his people. They had a sense of humor unfamiliar to him. When one told jokes, and others laughed, he was unsure what everyone was laughing about.

Bernard's mother, photographed on September 22, 1945.

Closer study revealed that the Puyallup Indians were having even harder times than his people. All of them seemed to be poor, more so than the Indians back home. He noticed that many of the children went without shoes. Some of the boys cut slits in their shoes so they could stretch and be worn for longer periods of time. When holes appeared in the soles of their shoes they placed a piece of leather or cardboard in the shoe to cover them.

The clothes they wore added to the appearance of poverty; most had patches. In some cases, the clothes were too small for the children who wore them. It was obvious that all the clothes were worn and old. He remembered that his white classmates in Okanogan were never dressed in this manner. This brought back thoughts of the differences between whites and Indians. These thoughts had occurred often to Bernard as he was growing up on and near the Colville Reservation. Now in Tacoma the poverty seemed worse.

He noticed that the houses the Puyallup lived in around Portland Avenue were in very poor shape and in need of repairs. Bernard could relate to this type of poverty. He had lived it most of his young life. But despite their poverty, he found the Puyallup were a friendly people, especially to Indians of other tribes. During this time, he made a number of friends among them.

While growing up on the reservation, then later in the town of Okanogan, the only people Bernard knew were either whites or Colville Indians. During those years, he experienced much poverty and, like others of his tribe, he was often hungry. There never seemed to be enough food. Milk and fresh vegetables were hard to come by. Fruit was unheard of high up in the mountains where his family lived. The only meat came when someone killed a deer or shot grouse and wild rabbits.

During the early forties, in the Manila Creek area near Keller, there was continuous news of the war on the radio. At an early age of four he seemed to understand what was going on with the war on more than one front. His dad and other adults in the area were surprised to see how much Bernard, at such a young age, knew of current events. They were further surprised when Bernard told them who the leaders of Germany, Japan, and Italy were. He had learned this from the many reports that came over the air.

As he grew, he was aware of his status in life and accepted being poor. He knew that others his age had more but he never let this deter him. He learned from his dad how to make ends meet, regardless of the situation. The poverty was never ending and continued into his high-school years. Whenever Bernard could find work, he took it eagerly. He was always grateful to those who offered him jobs and ways to help him make it through life.

Soon after his arrival in Tacoma, Bernard realized that Indians hung out on only one block of Tacoma, between 13th and 14th Streets on lower Pacific Avenue. The only other people that inhabited the block were soldiers from Fort Lewis, located fifteen miles south of Tacoma. They frequented the taverns usually occupied by Indians. It was obvious they were looking for girls and having a good time doing it.

Bernard could see that the only places of business there were three taverns, two pawnshops, a small theater and an arcade full of games designed for young people. It was noticeable that the stores on the block were not in the same class as the ones uptown. Two storefronts appeared to be vacated. Throughout the day and late into the night, there was constant activity on the street.

One night Bernard went into one of the Indian taverns called the J&M. Since he was only eighteen, he wanted to see if he could be served a beer. When he sat on a stool at the bar, he was pleased that the bartender ignored his age and brought him a bottle of Olympia. Bernard lit a cigarette and viewed the other customers in the tavern. He was not surprised to see that almost all of them were Indians. After a few beers, he had to go to the men's room. He had to sidestep to avoid puddles of urine that surrounded the two urinals there. As he stood within reach of one urinal, he read the graffiti on the wall in front of him. He guessed that most of it was written by servicemen of the past that were stationed at Fort Lewis during the war. He found much of the writing humorous. He laughed out-loud when he read, "In case of an air raid hide under the urinal. It hasn't been hit yet."

Returning to the bar, he noticed a large Indian seated at the end, drinking a beer. He remembered seeing him before at Harry Wong's restaurant. Bernard could sense the man was unusual, and of some importance. He moved closer to him and within minutes they were engaged in conversation.

The large man was a Puyallup Indian who had lived in Tacoma all his life where he fished for salmon in the Puyallup River. He introduced himself as Bob Satiacum. Bernard found the man interesting. That evening he would learn much about the coastal Indian culture. That chance meeting would prove to be an event that would eventually direct Bernard's life. As time went on, Bernard and the man became

81

When Bernard's tour of duty with the 101st Airborne
was completed, he joined Bob Satiacum as a fisherman on the Puyallup River. Courtesy: Lawney Reyes

close friends and met regularly at one of the taverns on Pacific Avenue. Bernard
would learn much about the problems the Puyallup Indians and the other tribes
in the area were facing in order to maintain their rights to fish for salmon.

During the following weeks, Bernard spent most of his time searching for
work. After a month of walking the streets, he learned that finding a job would be
impossible. He learned later that Indians were seldom hired and could only find
work in the raspberry fields near Puyallup. He did not find that idea attractive.
He had spent his summers and early fall working in the apple orchards, harvesting
other fruits and vegetables. He was tired of that type of work.

After learning that a number of his friends back home in Okanogan had
joined the armed services, he decided to leave Tacoma and join the army.
He knew he could get the GI Bill and have enough money to go to college.
After spending sixteen weeks at boot camp in Fort Ord, he decided to join
the 101st Airborne at Fort Campbell, Kentucky, where he knew he could
get higher pay. He soon adjusted to the intensive training and grew to love
the challenges of jump school. He could not wait to make his first parachute
jump. After extensive training, he became a Green Beret.

When his tour of duty was up in 1959, Bernard returned to Tacoma and stayed with his mother and sister, Luana, on Portland Avenue. It was not long before he ran into Bob Satiacum once again. The man was pleased to see Bernard. As they visited, Satiacum learned that Bernard had hopes of finding a job.

He studied Bernard and finished his beer. "Good luck! But I think you'll see it's still hard to find work here. Indians have always been denied jobs in Tacoma. If you don't find anything, look me up. I might be able to help you."

Bernard searched for weeks, but the employers he contacted showed little or no interest in hiring him. Bernard was disappointed with the results. One night, he went to the J&M and saw that Satiacum was already there, having a beer with one of his brothers, Buddy. Bernard joined them.

Satiacum ordered a round of beers, then suggested that Bernard fish with him on the river. When Bernard revealed he didn't know a thing about fishing with nets, Satiacum told him he would teach him all he needed to know. He would let him use a net and borrow a canoe and a motor. Satiacum could see that Bernard was grateful for the chance to make a little money. As time went on, he saw that Bernard was a fast learner and a hard worker. From then, Bernard learned the rudiments of coastal Indian fishing. He became a regular, fishing alongside Satiacum his two brothers, Buddy and Junior, and a friend, The Quinault, who had returned from Taholah for the new season.

During his time out on the water with his friends, Bernard learned much about what went on in the river and the Bay. The Quinault spent a lot of time explaining the nature of the salmon. He educated Bernard about the different species. He explained what time of the year they made their runs. The Quinault went into detail on how to place the drift net in the water to corral the salmon for better catches. He told Bernard that you could always tell when salmon hit the net by watching the cork floats. If the floats bobbled or sank, that was a signal a salmon was caught. The Quinault also explained how important it was to shake the net thoroughly to rid it of the jelly fish that had been caught. He went on to say that salmon would avoid approaching the net if jelly fish were present. Bernard found all of this very interesting and he became an avid pupil, always willing to learn more.

One night, as Satiacum stood along the shoreline, he watched as Bernard came floating down the Puyallup in his canoe. The fish were not running that night. There was a strong wind and from time to time it forced the waves to whip and tip the canoe. Bernard had just pulled the net into the canoe and proceeded to walk over it to get to the bow. As he was doing so, his foot caught on a part of the net and he tripped and fell into the river. It was icy cold. Satiacum and The Quinault saw this happen. As Bernard struggled to pull himself into the canoe Satiacum yelled, "Come on in. There's no fish tonight. Let's go to the Anchor and get something to drink. You had better get some place warm and try to dry out. You might freeze your tail if you don't."

Later that night, as they were sitting in the Anchor, Bernard still wet and cold, complained, "Damn, it's cold out there. That's my third time in the water in the last two weeks. Fishing is a hell of a way to make a living. It's hard to balance yourself in those damned canoes. Trying to make yourself comfortable on those little wood seats is hell on your ass. Once you fall in, it's nearly impossible to get back into the canoe. Look at my hands; they're so covered with calluses that I have a hard time just bending my fingers."

The Quinault shared, without smiling, "In time, you'll learn how to do it right. Just remember, the fisherman's place is in the canoe and the fish's place is in the water. The sooner you learn that the better off you'll be." Everyone laughed.

As time went on, each day and night mirrored the one before it. Time became predictable for those who fished. During the weekends everyone could expect the harassment of the white sportsmen. When day turned into night, the Tacoma police were always in their patrol boats looking for infractions. They always directed their attention to the Indian fishermen.

Fishing continued through the following weeks. Although Bernard tried, he did not have the ability to catch much salmon. But he made enough to live modestly and pay for his share of beer when he met the others at the taverns. Bernard appreciated living with his mother, Mary, on Portland Avenue. She had provided a bedroom and he was grateful; since he left the 101st Airborne he had been living from hand to mouth. More than once he thought about re-enlisting. Bernard thought it would be an easier way to make a living.

Before boarding his canoe one night, he watched Satiacum and the others as they drifted down the river. The only noise came from the activity of people and cars on Pacific Avenue. As Bernard watched his friends, it was like stepping back into an earlier century. They appeared almost ghostlike as they drifted quietly down the river. It occurred to him that Indians of the past probably gathered in the exact spot centuries ago. He suspected they probably fished in the same manner, out of carved canoes using hand-made nets, and probably spears. Bernard thought the only difference was no one had motors in the old days. He wondered if those of the past had any idea what their offspring would be going through in today's world.

He experienced a chilling feeling, as if spirits were guiding his thoughts. He felt he was a part of others long ago. He wondered if Satiacum and his crew, whom he thought of as fish Indians, had ever felt the same way. He wondered if the salmon in the river sensed they were a part of a chain of events and were instrumental in helping their two-legged cousins, the Puyallup, survive.

He could see that Indians had not really changed that much since those early times; there were a number of reasons. First, the whites who had come to the area denied the Indians from becoming a part of their culture and progress. But aside from that, he realized the Indians really didn't want to change. They were, and would always be, happy with their own way of life. As Bernard stood there, he found his reasoning and conclusions acceptable. He found the Puyallup Indian culture unique, something he was beginning to understand.

One Sunday, in late summer, Bernard drove to Fife where Satiacum lived. He had been invited to help patch damaged fishnets in preparation for the fall runs of salmon. The Quinault would be there and Bernard heard he was an expert at doing that kind of work. Earlier, when Bernard met the man for the first time, he was impressed with him and looked forward to getting to know him better. Satiacum provided smoked salmon and beer for the enjoyment of everyone. Never a person to turn down a free meal or free booze, Bernard eagerly accepted.

Later, Satiacum went into his house and exited into the backyard, followed by a curious cat. The cat was obviously an alley cat that had survived many battles. It looked as tough as the large rats that occupied the waterfront. Satiacum carried a half-filled can of Budweiser, his favorite beer. Under his other arm he carried a slab of baked salmon eggs, a delicacy to Puyallup Indians. That day Bernard, after some effort, learned to accept this new food with the rest of his friends.

"Ready to go to work? We're going to make an Indian fisherman out of you yet," Satiacum joked. "That's the first order of business before becoming a journeyman."

He laughed as he placed the salmon and fish eggs on top of one of the canoes. He turned and shouted to his wife, "Myrt, bring out more beer from the fridge. It should be cold enough now."

When Myrt appeared with a six-pack of Olympia, Bob introduced her to his little friend. Bernard could see that she was very attractive. Satiacum told Bernard that his wife was also a Quinault. "She's the same tribe as that guy over there working on the nets. He's the best fisherman on the river but Myrt is the best cook when it comes to salmon."

Bernard saw The Quinault, already at work repairing nets at the far end of Satiacum's backyard. He was impressed at how fast he worked. It was obvious that he had accomplished this task many times. He had a cigarette in his mouth and nodded at Bernard from across the yard. Satiacum brought Bernard over so he could see firsthand how the quiet man did his work.

That afternoon Bernard, Satiacum and The Quinault repaired nets as they drank beer. Later, Bernard learned much about fishing for salmon with nets as The Quinault shared his knowledge of the river and the fish that were in it. Bernard quickly learned about repairing nets and casting them into the water. The Quinault was a good teacher.

Before everyone left to prepare for a night of fishing, Bernard saw an axe handle leaning against a wall of a shed. He asked Satiacum if he could use it. Satiacum nodded, "Why do you want it?" Bernard answered, "I can't afford a shotgun like yours. If we have trouble out on the water with those white guys, it might come in handy." Satiacum grinned.

As evening approached, Bernard learned of the many problems the Puyallup were having on the river and Commencement Bay. Bernard could see the only real problem was the whites, who thought they owned the water and everything in it. He was beginning to wonder how he would cope with trouble if it got worse. He thought it would be better if the Indians had greater numbers when the time came. Bernard also thought that placing the axe handle close to him while in the canoe might help him through the night.

One night, as he sat in the J&M with Satiacum and The Quinault, Bernard asked, using one his favorite slang expressions for white people, "How are we going to deal with all this bullshit from the Suyapes? It's getting a little tiring. They never seem to let up. For as long as I can remember, that's the word my tribe has used when speaking about whites."

Satiacum smiled and thought awhile. "They're trying to wear us down. They think that after enough of their harassment we'll get tired and give up. They're waiting for that to happen. It's always been like this when we drift into the Bay. When the time comes that we need help, others who fish upriver will come to support us.

"The whites know how valuable the salmon are and they will not give up any day soon." Satiacum continued. "We're going to have to go along with the game they're playing. As far as I'm concerned, we're not going to give up either. We'll play with them as long we have to. We know the value of salmon but not only in dollar value. We know the importance they have to the tribe and all the people that are here now and those who will come in the future."

Bernard took off his coat and lit a cigarette. "Do you think we'll some day reach an agreement with the whites? Do you think we'll ever get to the point of sharing the salmon so that everyone is satisfied?"

Satiacum smiled and shook his head, "I don't think that will ever happen. They want all of the salmon and, as their numbers grow, it will get worse. We are too different. Indians really have nothing in common with their way of living. Our cultures are too far apart."

Satiacum ordered another round of beer. "Most whites treat 'Mother Earth' in a different way. They seem to have no respect for the land or anything that lives on the land. Look at what they have done since they first came here. There is nothing but destruction and pollution. They are either unaware of what they are doing or they don't care. I have no use for such people."

Bernard enjoyed listening to Satiacum as he talked about things of interest to him. He always seemed to make sense. He could find no holes in Satiacum's logic. His thinking was well grounded. Satiacum was eight years older than Bernard and he had acquired an understanding of life that Bernard had not thought of before. It seemed to Bernard that Satiacum was echoing the wisdom of the past, possibly his forefathers. There seemed to be much truth to what he was saying.

In contrast, the white sportsmen's reasoning seemed superficial and self-serving. There was no depth or feeling that could be connected to the welfare of others or other things, especially the environment. Their words seemed shallow and hollow.

As Bernard fished, he was always surprised at what lived in the water. Back home in eastern Washington what one could find in the streams, lakes and rivers became predictable. But at the mouth of the Puyallup river and Commencement Bay, he found sea-life that he had never seen before. After weeks of fishing, he learned that there were a number of species of salmon unknown to him. In addition to the coho and chinook, there were chum and humpback.

He was amazed when he caught his first sand shark. As he studied the fish, he was told by Satiacum that a friend of his had caught a large tiger shark that weighed about 380 pounds. When he thought of the many times he had fallen in the water, he was thankful that it happened when large sharks were not around. He was also interested in the jellyfish and he learned painfully to avoid the red ones. When Satiacum told him that at times blackfish came into Commencement Bay, Bernard was very surprised and hoped that one day he would have the opportunity to see one.

Bernard was pleased he was fishing with Satiacum and the others. It seemed to him they were engaged in something important, something worth fighting for. Indian fishing for salmon seemed more than earning money, or getting something to eat. To Bernard, it had a great deal more depth than that. It had something to do with fighting for rights. Bernard knew he would like to be a part of such a cause. By being here, he hoped he could help make a difference.

One night Satiacum and Bernard stood on the shore and watched The Quinault drift by.

His net was already out in the water and it was very quiet and still. He looked almost ghostly as he floated with the tide.

"The Quinault knows the patterns and movements of fish better than anyone I know," Satiacum said quietly.

"I wish I knew what he knows," Bernard quipped. "All I know is my catch is always the lowest. It's no secret that I still don't know a damn thing about fishing in this way."

"I remember you guys from east of the mountains lost all your fish in the late thirties, when the Grand Coulee Dam was built. Most of you probably don't even know what a salmon looks like today, or tastes like." Satiacum pulled his net from the water and shook the jellyfish loose. "The one thing in your favor is you guys don't have anything left the white boys like. In their eyes you no longer have anything of value. So they leave you alone. We still have fish over here and they want them all. That's why we have to fight just to get our share."

One afternoon, just before darkness, Satiacum called Bernard on the telephone. He asked if he would like to attend a meeting. Bernard accepted but did not know what he was getting into that evening at seven.

Bernard was already waiting for Satiacum when he arrived, smoking a cigarette. They drove to the northern part of the city, found the building and parked. As he and Bernard entered the large hall, they could hear people talking. It was filled with at least one hundred fifty white men seated in folding chairs. Satiacum could see that Bernard was surprised and sensed trouble when he realized all were white Sportsmen.

As they stood in the back of the room, Bernard whispered, "Are we in the right place? These guys don't seem very friendly."

The man chairing the meeting acknowledged them. "It looks like we have some unexpected visitors. Clear a place for them in the front row and let them sit down. Let's show them how gracious our people can be."

The two were seated directly in front of the speaker. Bernard could see clearly how determined the whites were in stopping Indian fishing. He could see that many were surprised and angered by the presence of two Indians. One after another got up to voice their feelings. They pointed their criticisms directly at Satiacum. Bernard recognized a number of them who had fished the Bay. They eyed Satiacum and Bernard with contempt. He remembered seeing them in their boats as they fished.

Satiacum could see that Bernard was distraught and nervous at being there. Satiacum smiled. He could plainly see that the whites did not like them and had a difficult time tolerating their presence. It was obvious as a number of them voiced their opinions of Indian fishing. They truly believed the Indians were the culprits because they were taking more salmon than the law allowed.

A half hour into the meeting, Satiacum suggested they leave. He thanked the chairman for allowing them to attend. The chairman asked if they had anything to say before they left.

Showing no concern or apprehension, Satiacum stood and answered, "I don't have much to say at this time. Now I know what is bothering all of you. But this will be settled one day in court. There is no question in my mind that we are in the right and we will win. Actually, as far as I'm concerned, this was settled over a hundred years ago when the Medicine Creek Treaty was signed."

There was angry grumbling in the crowd as Satiacum and Bernard left the room. Bernard was surprised that Satiacum had contained his composure. He showed no signs of alarm. He conveyed the feeling that everything was well in hand and he had done what he had come to do. Thinking there might be some rough stuff, Bernard backed out of the room just to be on the safe side, wishing he had brought his axe handle.

As Satiacum drove back to Pacific Avenue, Bernard could see that he did not have a care in the world at what went on earlier. He turned on his radio to listen to some rock and roll and tapped his forefinger on the steering wheel to keep time with the music.

Bernard blurted out, "Christ, are you crazy? I didn't think we were going to get out of that place alive. Did you see how pissed off those guys were?" Satiacum just grinned. It was obvious he enjoyed dealing with whites in his own way.

When they arrived at the J&M, Buddy and The Quinault were already enjoying their third beer. "Where were you guys?" Buddy asked. "I was beginning to think you weren't going to fish tonight."

Still noticeably shaken, Bernard replied, "It's lucky we're here at all. Your brother took me to white man's country tonight. Now I know how Custer felt when he saw Crazy Horse and Gall coming up the hill to pay their respects and lift his hair." Still flustered, Bernard shook his head and ordered another beer.

As weeks turned into months, Bernard learned that fishing for salmon, as his friends did, was not only hard work but dangerous. Survival every day and night, out on the water, required diligence and care. Bernard hoped he would have the discipline and strength to survive the ordeal. But he was pleased with all that he had learned. He knew he would never trade those experiences for anything. In spite of the hard times, he learned important ways of becoming a better man. He was pleased in learning how good salmon tasted by the unique methods of preparing them. He found when the salmon was baked secured to stakes driven into the ground surrounding a fire of limbs of alder, the flavor could not be beat.

When he lived east of the mountains, he never had the chance to enjoy salmon. Now that he lived on the coast, he found he could not get enough. After several weeks, he finally learned to appreciate baked salmon eggs, more so then when he first tried them. That was something he thought would never happen.

Later that night, Bernard and Satiacum met at the launching site of the river. A storm had been brewing and as darkness fell, it got worse. Strong winds came and it began to rain heavily. The waves in the river became extremely choppy. "I think I'll take off tonight after I tie down the canoes," Bob said. "The others have already wrapped it up. I think they'll be in the taverns. I'm going to join them. I think tonight will be a good time to be indoors where it's warm and dry."

Bob advised, "If you feel up to it, this might be the night when the runs will be heavy. If you stick it out, you might make some money. I think the wind will make the water rough, so don't fall into the river. This wouldn't be the night to do that."

Bernard decided to give it a try. He did need the money. He lit a cigarette and watched as Satiacum drove off. He checked his net, boarded his canoe, and paddled out to the center of the river. Because of the strong wind and heavy rain, he decided not to light the lantern, fastened to the inner tube, at the end of the net.

Within minutes, the weather got worse and the rain fell in sheets. Bernard had to continually bail water from the canoe with a gallon can. He was worried that the heavy rain might fill the canoe and swamp it. He was grateful that he had rain-gear. At least he could stay relatively dry. The life jacket he wore helped to keep him warm. As he fished, he wondered what the hell he was doing out on the water in this kind of weather.

He tried to steady the canoe as it drifted; the strong wind was continually moving it off course. Unexpectedly, the chinook hit. They came so fast and with such force that Bernard thought they would pull the net and the canoe beneath the surface. Within seconds, the net was full and the floats were pulled beneath the surface of the churning water. It took all of his strength to guide the canoe to shore. As he removed the fish from the net, he was surprised at their number. These were the largest chinooks he had ever seen. He guessed that a half dozen were over fifty pounds.

Bernard thought he would make the most of it that night and continued to drift. On his third drift, the wind blew him off balance and he fell into the water. It took all of his strength to get back into the canoe. He was thankful for the life jacket. Bernard knew he could have drowned without it. He had to sit for minutes just to get his wind and strength back, cold and soaked to the bone.

He decided to call it a night. When he studied the pile of chinook on the bank he could not believe how many he had caught. He could not have been more satisfied. Before crawling into the back seat of his car to get some sleep, he removed his wet clothing and wrapped himself into an old sleeping bag. Soon, he was asleep.

A night later, Bernard joined The Quinault at the J&M. The two sat for a few minutes enjoying their beer and watching others in the tavern. There was a good representation of Indians there from several tribes. There were also a number of very attractive girls, and the two men sat and enjoyed watching them as they made their way up and down the aisles, swaying their hips as they walked. Both wondered what tribes they came from and both agreed they would like to get to know them better.

The Quinault studied Bernard as they sat there, enjoying a cigarette. "Now that you are a regular, how do you like fishing for salmon? I understand you guys, east of the mountains, don't have them anymore, since Coulee Dam went in."

Bernard set his cigarette aside in the ashtray. "It's hard work and dangerous. It seems that half the time I'm in the water. It's a good thing I'm a good swimmer. Its hard as hell getting back into the canoe once you fall in." He paused. "The thing I dislike the most is the wet cold and the smell. Even when I sit in a tub for an hour I still can't get rid of the fishy smell. Also, those damn red jellyfish. They can really sting."

The Quinault smiled. "In time, you'll get used to it. You'll learn to cope with everything when you fish. Cut open a lemon and rub yourself with it. It helps with the smell. When you pull in your net make sure you wear gloves. That will help with the jellyfish."

During another evening, Bernard learned that The Quinault had a unique sense of humor. As they were drinking, The Quinault leaned forward and asked in his low-keyed voice, "Have you ever heard of Qweets?"

Bernard thought a while and answered, "Isn't that the little community, on the coast, just north of Taholah? I have never been there but friends of mine told me about it. Why?"

The Quinault paused, lit a cigarette and asked, "Do you know how that place got its name?"

Bernard shook his head, wondering.

"Well, over a hundred years ago, the Spanish army sent troops up along the Pacific coast to explore the area. They were having a very hard time along the way because of heavy brush and rough terrain that had no trails. One time, after a very hard day, one of the soldiers, who was completely exhausted, sat down on the trunk of a fallen tree and wiped the sweat from his brow. He told the others, "I'm getting sick and tired of all this bullshit exploring. For Christ sakes, let's go home now and call it Qweets.""

At first, Bernard missed the point, but when he finally got it, he had to bend over from laughing so hard.

Before Bernard could finish laughing, The Quinault had another story to share. He whispered, "I have to tell this one about Joe DelaCruz, our tribe's leader. I think you know him." Bernard nodded. "One night a bunch of us got together in a tavern near Hoquiam. There were about five of us with Joe who had just bought a pair of new cowboy boots. Another guy walked in a few minutes later and as Joe was crossing his legs, he saw the boots. The guy admired them and asked, 'Are those Tony Lamas?' Joe looked at him, a bit taken aback, then showing annoyance, answered. 'Hell no, they're mine.'"

Again Bernard laughed and blurted out, "That's a good one. I'm going to have to remember it. For the life of me, I didn't know Joe was so damned uninformed."

The Quinault ground out his cigarette in an ashtray and stood. "It's getting late. I think the fish might make their runs tonight. Let's go fishing." Bernard nodded, put on his coat, and followed the slender man to his car, knowing The Quinault could read the behavior of salmon better than anyone.

Later, out on the river, The Quinault's predictions proved correct. The salmon hit the nets hard for about an hour. Bernard, under the direction of the quiet man, easily caught his share of fish. He had caught several silvers and made enough money to last him a week.

During early morning, the buyers came and purchased every fish the Indians caught. Satiacum came by to see how his men did and was pleased with the amount of fish they caught. He had brought five thermoses of hot coffee and a sack full of donuts. The five finished their breakfast as they sat on the bank of the river. They knew the whites would soon appear on the Bay, and noise and confusion would begin. All were tired. They were too tired to go to their homes, so they crawled into their cars to get a few hours' worth of sleep.

In the spring of that year, the life of Bernard Reyes began to change. He had applied for a job at the Boeing Company in Seattle. He was surprised when he received a letter in the mail four weeks later. He had been hired. He was pleased to hear this and called Satiacum, his brothers, and The Quinault to join him at the Milwaukee Tavern on Pacific Avenue for a celebration. That evening, Buddy toasted Bernard and told him he was relieved that he had finally gotten a real job. Buddy was tired of fixing Bernard's motor out on the river every time it needed repairs. "I used to wonder if you could repair your old car, why, in hell couldn't you repair that little motor on the canoe?"

Junior informed everyone that it was good that Bernard landed a job doing something else because he couldn't see how anyone could survive with the amount of money he made on the river.

Bernard laughed and agreed. During the years of fishing, Bernard was always low man on the totem pole when it came to catching fish. The Quinault smiled quietly as he offered to buy the second round of beer. He lit a cigarette and shared, "I have never met anyone who has fallen in the river as much as you. You guys from eastern Washington must like to swim, even in freezing weather." Everyone laughed.

The job at Boeing proved good for Bernard. For the first time in his life, he opened a checking account of a modest amount and was able to save a little money. He met a number of white people he liked. He learned the ropes and steadily progressed. A number of his co-workers were more than willing to help him. Bernard was happy he could now pay his way.

One Sunday, Satiacum called and invited Bernard to sit in on a meeting he had scheduled for later in the day. He was curious what Satiacum had in mind. Then he thought about the first meeting he had with him when they attended the one with all the sportsmen. Bernard wondered if it would be as precarious as that one.

As Bernard drove into the parking lot located south of the Puyallup cemetery, he could see a number of buildings that turned out to be Satiacum's headquarters. Bernard noticed that a number of the men who worked for Bob carried concealed handguns. Satiacum gave him a tour of the premises. Bernard was surprised to see a long rack of over a dozen and a half carbines fully loaded and ready for use. Next to them were several boxes of ammunition. It reminded him of his days with the 101st Airborne at Fort

Campbell. He could see that Satiacum was prepared for any problems that might come from any of his detractors.

When he sat with Satiacum in his office having a beer, Bernard could see that his friend still had his twelve-gauge pump leaning against the wall close to his desk, within easy reach. From a window, he could see a number of Satiacum's men walking about the parking lot, ever watchful for any suspicious activity. He could see that they all carried handguns in shoulder holsters.

About a dozen men entered the room to attend the meeting. After everyone was seated, Satiacum stood and shared his plans. "For the past few days, I have been thinking about setting a blockade across I-5 where the reservation boundary is." Bernie could see the instant interest displayed in the eyes of everyone there. "I think it's time that we start charging a toll to everyone who passes through our land. We should have thought of this a long time ago, so I think the time has come."

A Negro attorney by the name of Tanner spoke up with apprehension as his eyes widened. "Am I hearing you right? Do you intend to put up a blockade across the I-5 freeway?" Satiacum nodded. Tanner's eyes widened further and he continued, "How in hell do you intend to enforce it?"

Satiacum finished his Coors and tossed the empty beer can into a wastebasket. He tapped his twelve-gauge, "With guns!"

Bernard was not only surprised with Satiacum's answer but he was surprised at seeing a can of Coors beer. He had heard that the beer was brewed in Colorado and was not allowed for sale in Washington state. He wondered how Satiacum was able to get the beer. Bernard smiled when he saw how Satiacum kept it cold. It was stored in a Coke machine that had to be kicked to retrieve one.

It was obvious that everyone at the meeting expressed concern with Satiacum's idea. They were not sure if he was serious. They were not sure if they wanted to be a part of this. Satiacum could see the uneasiness of everyone and smiled. "I can see that all of you have problems with this, so I'm going to table it for now but I want all of you to think about it. There could be a lot of money involved if we do it. We'll meet in a few days to go over it in more detail. OK?"

Satiacum's idea left everyone stunned. His proposal was met with dead silence. All wondered if it would work. The idea seemed logical but would it work and could it be enforced with guns? Would it be legal? Bernard thought if Satiacum blockaded I-5, where the bridge passed over the Puyallup River, marking the Puyallup Reservation boundary, it would create one hell of a traffic jam, probably all the way up to the Canadian border. He smiled at such a thought and wondered how Satiacum could come up with such ideas. There were many concerns and questions going through everyone's minds as they left the meeting that evening. It was obvious that everyone was unsettled.

Within time, Bernard found an apartment near his family, now living on Beacon Hill in Seattle, just a few miles south of city center. His place of work at Boeing was only three miles from where he lived. To get the exercise he needed, and to save money on gas, he would jog to work. Since he worked the swing shift, he enjoyed the run during the evening hours when the weather was not too hot.

Although Bernard had many friends in Tacoma and liked it there, he often thought the challenges in Seattle might be more important. He knew that many Indians were now moving into the city from other tribes. Because Seattle was a liberal city, he felt if he was going to do something important for the welfare of his people, he would have a better chance in doing it there. There was just too much prejudice against minorities in Tacoma, especially against Indians. He had definitely learned this firsthand.

6. Su'Zan

DURING HER EARLY YEARS, life was not easy for Susan Eads. All of her time was spent searching for her identity and her acceptance. Her parents never took the time to help her grow and learn in those early years. In the beginning, she was shuffled from one relative to the other on her father's side. No one in that family displayed any interest in her. There was never any love and commitment shared when she needed it most.

During those pre-teen years, Susan experienced feelings of loss and separation. She never had the chance to make long-lasting friends her age. At times, she thought of her parents and she missed their brief times together. At first those were good times and she wished that those good times could have lasted longer. Her father was an officer in the U.S. Army and they traveled constantly from one military post to another. The family was never able to establish roots for long in one place. Her father was white but he was also a member of the Kaw tribe that once lived in Kansas. Susan's mother was Elvina Sampson, a member of the Upper Skagit tribe in western Washington, near Bellingham. She was also half Norwegian. Susan was the only child, and the family struggled to maintain itself with their way of living. Soon the pressures of marriage began to tell on Susan's mother. Quarrels between her father and mother became commonplace. It was difficult for Susan to cope with the situation at home.

Afterwards, she was sent to the small community of LaConner, Washington, by her mother. There she met two of her mother's sisters, Helen and Ida. While there she still felt out of place. Later, she was sent to Tacoma. Life proved better for Susan when she met her Aunt Margaret Hook, also her mother's sister. Aunt Margaret invited her to live with her family in a rented house on Portland Avenue in Tacoma.

While growing up on Portland Avenue, Susan had difficulty making friends her own age. Again she began to feel uncomfortable while living with her Aunt Margaret and her family. She felt like an outsider. It bothered her to think that she was adopted. But she did get on well with Joyce Meachem, her first cousin, who was four years older. During this time Joyce tried to make life easier for Susan. She took on the responsibility of raising her and teaching the ways of life that her mother should have taught. Susan grew to admire Joyce. She could see that her cousin was very attractive, intelligent, and caring. During that time, the two became very close.

Susan was of a fair complexion; she was often mistaken as white, especially when she entered high school. She once remarked, "I didn't look Indian. I was dating a classmate who was Indian at the time and some of his white friends asked him why he wasn't going out with an Indian girl."

"She is an Indian, just like me," he answered.

"From then on I might as well have had a social disease as far as the white kids were concerned," she remarked.

While still a teenager of sixteen, Susan met Bob Satiacum. She finally found someone she felt she could trust. They got along well, and she became interested in how he made his living. She found it exciting being out on the water of the Puyallup River and Commencement Bay in an Indian canoe and experiencing a feeling of being completely free. With ease, she learned and accepted Satiacum's way of life and methods of catching fish. She often went out with him to cast the long nets he carried for netting salmon. Soon, she became expert at casting them herself. From that time on, she began to enjoy a new way of life.

One time, while fishing in the Yakima area, Satiacum needed help in delivering the salmon he caught to market. He asked Susan to drive a truck full of salmon to the Crown Seafood Market on the waterfront in Seattle. Susan was greatly surprised, and responded, "I don't know how to drive cars, much less trucks. Besides that, I don't have a license."

Su'Zan Satiacum learned the art of net fishing at the earky age of sixteen. Courtesy: © Bob Peterson

Satiacum responded, "I don't have much time, we don't have time to quibble; I can teach you what you need to know in a few minutes."

After some difficulty and much time, Susan finally reached Snoqualmie Pass. Because the salmon were not packed in boxes, every time she went around a curve they slid to the other side of the cab rocking the truck severely. This made it difficult for Susan to maintain control of the truck. Hours later, she finally reached Crown Seafood to find they didn't need any more salmon. She called Satiacum and he suggested she take the load to a market in Portland, Oregon.

While in Seattle, Susan was caught in a rainstorm. She was left standing on the sidewalk, dripping wet and shivering, without shoes. Ivar Haglund, a Seattle legend, saw her and realized she needed help. He walked up and invited her into his famous restaurant to dry out and get warm. Afterwards, he treated her to a free salmon dinner. Susan was forever grateful for the kindness offered by

Ivar. She never forgot him. She was now a journeyman at delivering salmon, an entrepreneur at marketing fish, and an expert driver of large trucks.

During those times Susan learned of the hard times Satiacum was facing. It seemed that every time he caught salmon in the river, there was someone in uniform who would take it upon himself to confiscate the fish, harass, handcuff, and take him off to jail. At other times, tug-boat operators would purposefully direct their boats and mangle any nets they could find. This usually took place during the evening hours. When daylight came, there were hundreds of white sportsmen who harassed him by ramming his canoe, shouting obscenities or riding over and tangling his driftnet.

At the age of twenty, Susan married Satiacum. Although he had five children from his former marriage, she managed to care for them and was pleased with her role as a housewife. During those days, Satiacum spent most of his time on the water fishing, leaving Susan to care for the children and the household. But she didn't mind, she was happy that she now had a home of her own.

In time, other problems arose, and Susan decided to help her husband. She wanted to be at his side regardless of the pressures directed against him by white authorities. She had always been a person who believed in fair play and justice. She could now understand the prejudice and injustices the Puyallup Indians were facing in Tacoma at almost every level. Now that she had committed herself to this choice of action she thought it important to change her name. She decided to call herself Su'Zan because she thought it unique. Susan was pleased that her new name was her own invention, her own idea.

She and Satiacum now had two children of their own. It became quite a chore for the two to care and feed the seven children that now occupied their household. But all of the Puyallup fishermen were facing similar problems just surviving. To make things worse the sportsmen were now increasing the pressure on all Indians out on the water.

During this time, the state became more and more severe in the enforcement of the Fisheries Code, directed completely against the Indians. A number of businesses, including restaurants and grocery stores, began to show discourtesy to Indians when they came to trade. Because of this unfair treatment and the need to survive, more Indians became involved to fight for their inherent rights.

One time a white antagonist stated in front of the press, "Satiacum is the biggest thing since PT Barnum. He's out there preaching the gospel and getting all the liberals to shed tears over the Indians and all that time he's cleaning up. You know, one year he cleared $87,000 selling the fish he caught."

When Su'Zan heard this, she was outraged. "People really don't understand, or if they do, they won't admit it. They are never honest when they talk about Bob. They don't realize how many Indians depended on him. At one point, there were more than a hundred Indians that he was supporting. He had taken it upon himself to help his people. He lent them canoes with motors. He offered drift nets and money to get them through the hard times. He even marketed the fish for them on the banks of the river once they were caught."

There were marches to the state capitol in Olympia where Indians voiced their complaints. The Indians experienced a hard time getting the press involved. The newspapers in Tacoma refused to allow them to buy ads professing their rights. Even TV stations were reluctant to respond favorably to the Indians plight. The Indians could see no one in the Tacoma area was willing to take a stand on their behalf.

One day, while surrounded by the press, Su'Zan responded angrily. "The Medicine Creek Treaty was a federal treaty, not a state treaty. I don't see how a biased state judge can have the right to renegotiate the treaty. I thought only Congress in Washington DC could do that. After all, the grass still grows and the sun still shines in this area, and there are still fish in the Puyallup, no matter what white men have done to it. We've always fished the Puyallup, and it's what the treaty calls our usual and accustomed ground."

During the conflict with the whites, Su'Zan had engaged in a number of verbal battles. When she learned that the Puyallup Indians were paid only $32,000.00 for the land they lost, her resentment grew. She knew that totaled less than four cents an acre. Su'Zan would never fully understand the greed of the white man in the Tacoma area.

One time, while being interviewed, she was angered once more. "I don't understand the legal words the white men use. They have always used their language to fool Indians. But I know they didn't want to stop the Indians from fishing on account of conservation laws or problems that relate to it. They were just afraid of the Sportsmen because the members of that organization in this state are large and they are powerful."

Now Su'Zan was determined to get help wherever she could find it. She felt it was time to get help from the press. She approached the Tacoma News Tribune. She was aware that the Indians had never received any good ink covering their battles for their mainstay, their lifestyle. She tried a number of times but she was always denied.

One day to her surprise she received a call from Johnny Cash, the great country-western star. He told her he would be performing in Salem, Oregon; he had been hearing of the troubles the Indians were having in the Tacoma area. He invited her and Bob to come down to meet him. After meeting, Cash told them he would do what he could to help. Later, he came to perform in Seattle. After his performance, Johnny Cash treated Bob and Su'Zan to a special steak dinner at the El Gaucho Restaurant. Elaine Ward, the attractive owner of the restaurant, welcomed them warmly and made them feel at home. She had always believed in the cause of Indians and would do anything in her power to help them.

A few weeks later Su'Zan, still smarting from earlier conflicts with the law enforcement authorities, drove with some friends to Frank's Landing on the Nisqually river south of Tacoma. They wanted to watch a number of their friends from the tribe fish. While she was there she saw at least forty white men in uniforms hidden within the trees across the river. All were holding what appeared to be nightsticks that law enforcement officials carried.

When the Indians started to fish, the white authorities charged across the river in motorboats and began attacking the Indians: men, women, and young children. The Indians picked up long poles, rocks, and whatever else they could find and fought back. There were other whites, believed to be Sportsmen, who fought on the side of the officials. During the melee, Su'Zan saw a white man draw something from his back pocket. An Indian man wrestled it from him and Su'Zan saw that it was a blackjack made of lead and leather.

The fighting was vicious as both sides used clubs and poles to maim each other. The young children, seeing their parents greatly outnumbered and being beaten with nightsticks and brass knuckles, began to throw rocks at the authorities. The authorities, in turn, viciously slapped the young ones aside. As the fight continued, Su'Zan witnessed a white sportsman dragging a daughter of Al Bridges, who was only thirteen years old, by her hair. She could see that the girl's face was bloodied by someone who had punched her.

Su'Zan knew the wars the Nisqually fought against the whites were the same that the Puyallup fought. It was basically the fight for the right to fish for salmon. She fought bravely that day alongside the Nisqually.

The fight that ensued was vicious. The Indians thought the men they fought were agents from the Fish and Wildlife Services that were supported by a number of the white Sportsmen; a group of Nisqually fishermen were the target. But over half of the Indians were women and children. During the conflict, Paris Emery, an elderly white man of seventy-three years, had a movie camera and documented most of the fighting on film.

At one point three white officers grabbed Su'Zan and struggled to force her into the back seat of a patrol car. She fought back furiously, but they finally managed to push her into the car and close the door. Unfortunately, one of the officers was not able to get out of the car in time. Su'Zan punched him several times in the face; she kicked him hard in the groin before he managed to open the door and fall to the ground.

Many who knew Su'Zan were aware how tough she was, a force to be reckoned with at the height of five feet nine inches. Some thought the white man was lucky he wasn't killed or seriously injured while in the backseat.

Afterward, Su'Zan was overpowered and handcuffed by other law enforcement officers. She was taken to Olympia and placed in a jail cell with a number of other Indian women who had fought alongside her. This would be just one of numerous times in her life that she would spend time behind bars.

When the Puyallup Indians heard about this, they were deeply concerned. After some of them viewed Paris Emery's film of the encounter, their anger bordered on rage. It showed, graphically, the violence that resulted on the bloody faces of their friends as they fought large numbers of whites who came to teach the Indians a lesson. One could predict there would be more trouble in the future.

The following months proved extremely difficult for both the Puyallup and Nisqually Indians. Su'Zan stated angrily, "After that fight, I knew what we could expect from the authorities. I learned what politics was all about, about how you need power to get anything done. And about how we Indians don't have that power."

Later in another altercation, Su'Zan was severely beaten by over two dozen Sportsmen. Bruised and bloody, she went to the police station in Tacoma to file charges. After meeting with a prosecuting attorney, she was advised that she could not be helped. She was ordered to drop all charges because the city of Tacoma was being considered for the "All City Award." An attorney for the city added, "It would be embarrassing to the city if you insisted on filing the charges at this time."

Towards the end of 1965, it became impossible for Bob Satiacum or any of his fellow tribal members to fish the Puyallup River. Satiacum was aware that Billy Frank Jr. and the Nisqually were having the same problem on their river. If they were caught, they were arrested and put behind bars. The white authorities were determined to break the will of the Indian fishermen once and for all. They were confident the law, the courts and the press, designed by their own kind, would work in their favor. Whenever the Puyallup gathered in numbers to protest the treatment they were receiving, the Tacoma police were seen with rifles and scopes watching them closely from a distance.

Now the white authorities exercised strict control of Indian fishing. When Indians went to fish, they were immediately arrested. However, the authorities decided some leniency might be in order. To prevent complete starvation among the Indians, they agreed to let the women fish, but only to provide food for their families. But the women were only allowed to fish at night so as not to antagonize the Sportsmen. The authorities reasoned this method of fishing might soften the attitudes of the Sportsmen and lessen any conflicts that might occur as a result.

It was embarrassing for the Indians to accept this situation but they had no choice. Su'Zan had been trained by Satiacum in the ways of net-fishing, so she knew what she was doing. Other women in the Puyallup tribe did their best in assuming the roles of the men but they had difficulty catching the number of fish needed. They were not experienced and did not have the physical strength to deal with net fishing. Soon Satiacum and other Puyallup men, feeling sorry for the women, went out to fish to relieve them. Once again, this resulted in a large number of arrests.

The following months and years were difficult for the Puyallup and Nisqually Indians. Because it was hard to catch enough salmon, there was not enough to trade with the Yakimas in eastern Washington. This had always been their custom. Many of the families in these tribes had to go on rations to simply make it through the cold months. Most of them relied on the generos-

Su'Zan prepares a net for fishing as she goes to work in place of her husband, Bob. Courtesy: © Bob Peterson

ity and good will of the Yakima to make it through the winter without starving.

To make things worse, whites took the war right to the Indian's homes. One evening when Su'Zan and her children returned home, she found their dog lying near the front door with its head cut off. She was appalled and her children were heartbroken. Another time, she found garbage spread all over her front yard. One night, as she and her children were having their evening meal, someone drove by and fired two gunshots through the front door. From that time on, Su'Zan always kept a .38 special revolver within close reach.

One afternoon, just before dark, Su'Zan arrived at her house. As she started to unlock her door, she could hear noises inside. She peered through the blinds of a window and saw a man holding a gun inside. She ran to her car to get her .38-caliber pistol and fired into the door then took cover behind a tree. Someone fired back from inside. She was not planning to shoot anyone; she just wanted to make sure whoever was inside would not escape. She hoped the police would arrive after hearing the gunfire.

Within minutes the police arrived in three patrol cars, red lights flashing, the two men inside surrendered and were taken to jail. Su'Zan followed and when the police realized she was Satiacum's wife they became arrogant. When she saw that one of the men was hiding a sack that contained $45,000 of Satiacum's money, she asked that it be returned to her. The police refused and asked where the money came from. "From the sale of fireworks," Su'Zan responded. The police were somewhat surprised at the amount of money in the sack but they dismissed her immediately; the money was never returned.

As time passed, Su'Zan turned belligerent and defiant. She regarded the abuse Indians were experiencing as criminal. All elements of authority in Tacoma were treating the Indians with disrespect. She could not understand how they could place Indians in jail for simply trying to survive and feed their families.

Not all of the Puyallup supported Satiacum and Su'Zan in their plight. A number in the tribe were jealous and regarded Bob as a trouble-maker that threatened an unwritten truce with the whites that allowed Indians to exist in a hostile community.

"Exist!" Su'Zan shouted. "That's all it's been for us! That's all it'll ever be, unless there is somebody who can do something about it.

7. The Sportsmen

WHEN SATIACUM AND HIS BROTHERS, Buddy and Junior, were very young their father, Chester, would often share memories of the old days on the Puyallup River. "At that time, white fishermen were around on the Bay and the mouth of the river but there weren't that many of them. There was little trouble between them and us but later, as their numbers grew; bad times began. I remember when they formed this club, in 1934 if I remember right. I think they called themselves 'The Washington State Sportsmen Council'. We just called them Sportsmen. There has been nothing but trouble for us ever since."

Satiacum and his brothers listened carefully as their father spoke of those early days. They never tired of hearing stories about those times, many years before they were born. They would always remember the history of these foreigners after arriving in their homeland and how it changed the lives of their family.

"When they first got here, years before, I don't think they ever saw a salmon in their life. But after watching us Indians fish and smelling salmon cooking over an open fire, they became interested.

"They were surprised when they saw us Indians. At first, they were scared because of those Indian warriors who attacked them along the way west. They were happy to see that us around here weren't going to cause trouble. Whites found us interesting....you know, the way we lived. But all agreed, it could never measure up to the way they lived. They thought about us Indians as a people of the past, not a part of the world today."

107

Chester cherished this time spent with his sons.

As time passed , a number of whites built small boats and rowed out into the Bay to experiment with salmon fishing. They soon learned that salmon loved small herring, . They discovered the large salt-water Bay was filled with them. There was more than one species, also, and the fish made their runs up the river to spawn at different times of the year. The adventure of fishing in the river and the Bay became a pleasure and a pastime for many of the newcomers.

The number of white fishermen grew steadily over the years. Their love of salmon fishing in the Bay motivated them to form a club. All agreed the title of this new organization, formed in 1934, would be 'The Washington State Sportsmen's Council. The main purpose of their group claimed to be to protect the wildlife in the forests and the fish in the sea.

At first, the Indian fishermen were not considered to be a real threat to the whites or their fledgling organization. The two groups fished independently, ignoring the other. Bay. Once the whites learned to eat salmon, their favorites soon became the large chinook and the coho. Other species, such as the chum and the humpback were less acceptable, but they were caught mainly for the sport of it.

More whites grew to enjoy the adventure of fishing in salt water and looked upon it as a sport.. Most did not necessarily prefer eating salmon. When they caught them, they usually gave them to others who had grown accustomed to the taste. In time, this changed, and the fish gradually became acceptable for a growing number in the area.

Now, most believed that whites owned all the fish in what was called Commencement Bay because of their payment for permits and the fact that they were now in the majority. They believed no one had the right to tell them otherwise since the legislature in the state capital of Olympia echoed their feelings. At these meetings, the sentiments against Indians grew stronger.

During the mid-fifties, the Sportsmen noticed that the number of Indians who fished in the river were increasing. Most of the Indians fished upriver in the Puyallup with nets anchored to the shore. At first, little attention was paid to these natives. Most of the Sportsmen knew little about them. Only a few had ever talked to one. Many did not know of Indian tribes that lived in the area and were unaware of their history and background. All were ignorant of how the government dealt with them.

After a few Indian fishermen appeared drifting their nets from canoes close to the Bay, the whites now presented rules that Indians would be allowed to fish on the incoming river only. At first, the Indians were surprised, but soon accepted the change They had no desire to mingle with others who were strange to their ways. Since the Indians stayed on the river and never entered the Bay they were paid little heed by the whites. The Indians now fished during the night, they were seldom seen except during the early morning when they gathered the fish from the anchored nets along the shores of the river.

It became common, after a day of fishing, that storms of protest were voiced in the taverns on the Tide Flats. The whites agreed that they would have to control the fishing methods of the Indians. They felt if they allowed Indians to fish uncontrolled it would hurt and diminish the salmon runs for everyone. A decision to protest was enacted and eventually supported in the state capitol at Olympia. White fishermen now believed that laws would have to be drawn up to curtail all Indian fishing.

Soon the Tacoma Police were alerted and they began to patrol the Bay at night with ideas of harassing any Indian on the water after daylight. When Indians were caught fishing illegally in the Bay they were fined or taken to jail. This became common practice of the police force and made it difficult for the Indians to fish in their accustomed way.

Not all whites held animosity against the Indians; a number were willing to share the salmon. A few knew that the Medicine Creek Treaty granted that Indians could fish within their accustomed areas. This attitude was supported when a number of whites remembered when Director of Fisheries, Milo Moore, stated, "If any man or race of people merits consideration in a fishery beyond that of all others, the American Indians claim that right."

Although a number of whites felt this way, they never spoke up in support of the Indians. Years later, attitudes began to change within the white community. Many whites began to see the Indians had a case after fish-ins and demonstrations and positive newspaper articles, from other cities, appeared in favor of Indians. . Later, a number of non-Indian organizations, some from the University of Washington, including certain church groups, threw their support to the Indians.

109

Some whites were embarrassed with how a number of those in their organization behaved on the water. They did not feel it necessary to harass the Indian fishermen in an aggressive manner. It made them uncomfortable when derogatory words were hurled. They found it difficult to control the behavior of the aggressive whites on the water, so many chose to mind their own business and enjoy themselves simply by moving and catching salmon in other parts of the Bay.

Regardless of the positive feelings that some whites experienced, many who did not fish became convinced by reading the local newspapers that Indian fishing was hurting all salmon runs. They felt that efforts to sustain the runs would be difficult if Indian fishing was not curtailed. Eventually, hard feelings against Indian fishing shifted to negative feelings against all Indians.

It was during these years, in the early sixties, that war between the whites and Indians reached its peak. All Indians in Tacoma were now viewed with a degree of contempt and became welcome in only certain parts of the city.

Many whites believed that Indians should be squeezed out of Tacoma. They felt if jobs were withheld from them, the Indians would be forced to move elsewhere simply to survive. If they were ostracized in places of business and restaurants, this might compel them to trade elsewhere. A number of whites, who totally disregarded Indians as humans, felt this might be the best way to rid themselves of a form of lowlife that they did not want to understand and with whom they had nothing in common.

The Sportsmen felt the pressure they were exerting on Indians would soon pay off. Other whites, who lived in Tacoma, were beginning to feel the same way. They would support the Sportsmen even though they did not fish for salmon and did not belong to the organization.

The continued arrogant behavior of a growing number of Indians did not help things. The whites wanted to use whatever physical force that was necessary to correct the situation. Most did not believe in strong physical force that might lead to violence, but many continued to harass the Indians anyway.

At times, when the whites and Indians engaged in heated arguments on the Bay, there was some pushing and shoving when the boats of the whites and the canoes of the Indians got within reach of each other. Each side was careful not to let it go beyond that.

110

But then, unexpectedly, Sportsmen began to sense change. The Indian fishermen no longer left their nets unattended. They left young Indian boys, armed with baseball bats and steel pipes, to guard their supplies when they were not there; the boys were determined to do their job. The whites could see they meant business and did not force the issue. At other times, on the water, the whites were reluctant to press the Indians because they suspected they might be armed.

A number of Sportsmen became uncomfortable with these changes. No one could predict what the future would hold, but unbelievable forces were at work that would enhance the impoverished Indians' lifestyle and behavior, to the surprise of everyone.

On February 12, 1974, after years of struggle and confrontation with the Indians, Washington State Authorities and the Sportsmen were dealt a major setback. A white man, a United States district judge, came into prominence. This unpretentious man would change the lives of the western Washington Indians forever.

"He loved the law. He would not do
anything to violate his duties as judge."
– Judge Boldt's son

8. The Judge

GEORGE HUGO BOLDT was born on December 28, 1903, in Chicago. After graduating from the Montana School of Law in 1926, he began his practice as an attorney in Helena, Montana. Shortly afterward, he moved to Seattle, where he continued his private practice until 1940, when he served as a Washington State special deputy attorney general. When the United States entered World War 11, Boldt joined the U.S. Army and served as a lieutenant colonel until 1946. Afterwards he returned to the Tacoma area and resumed his private practice. He became a special prosecuting attorney for Pierce County in 1948 and later served as a federal judge to the United States District Court for the Western District of Washington.

On June 10, 1953, President Dwight D. Eisenhower nominated him to a seat vacated by Judge Charles H. Leavy. On July 14, 1953, Boldt was confirmed by the United States Senate and received his commission that same day. He served as chief judge until 1971 and then assumed senior status on October 30 of that year.

During this period in time, the Puyallup and Nisqually Indians were engaged in a heated war with the State of Washington. The fight was over the salmon in the Puyallup and Nisqually Rivers. When both the Indians and the whites began to notice declining fish runs, blame was eventually placed on the Indians and their methods of fishing. As time went on, problems got worse. The Sportsmen's association was growing larger and they began to exercise greater pressure on the Washington State Legislature to pass laws that would restrict Indian fishing.

Jack Tanner, an NAACP attorney, willingly made his time available to Bob Satiacum and other tribes in need of advice and support. He and his local group raised funds for the SAIA. He later became a federal judge.
Courtesy: Museum of History & Industry

Although Bob Satiacum and Billy Frank Jr. held center stage in the fight for Indian fishing rights in the State of Washington, other important involvements had been taking place. There were a number of other Indians and non-Indians who were working to make changes by getting outside support and having their voices heard. Their words and actions proved instrumental in obtaining federal recognition and support from other important non-Indian agencies and organizations that were concerned about civil rights.

Many well-known activist groups and concerned individuals joined the struggle as the Puyallup and Nisqually staged their fish-ins. Adept and thoughtful courtroom strategies had been provided by the National Association for the Advancement of Colored People (NAACP) lawyers, led by Jack Tanner, a Tacoma attorney. The American Civil Liberties Union (ACLU) and, finally, the U.S. Department of Justice made their weight felt as the battle waged on. After many demonstrations, protest marches, decisions of non-native judges, and the influence of changing public opinion, the Indians were finally getting close to their day in court.

114

When one studies the situation, the victories of the Puyallup and the Nisqually could not have been realized without the involvement of the Survival of the American Indian Association (SAIA), led by Janet McCloud, the NAACP and the National Indian Youth Council (NIYC). In truth, certain elements of the SAIA protest campaign were modeled after the black civil protests in the South. The NIYC was ably led by Hank Adams, a resident of Frank's Landing. The group pushed for greater recognition and strove for the rejection of cultural assimilation. This was in contrast to the goals of the black civil-rights movement. With the NIYC's new methods of protest and advocacy, a strong and independent Native American culture grew. Through their actions, this group elicited important responses from the media and other interested white organizations. They began to understand the truth and validity of the Indian's movement.

The SAIA and the NIYC were formed in the early 1960s to support the Indians who fished for decades and were harassed continually by white

Hank Adams was an Indian rights activist who was instrumental in working to protect Indian fishing rights. He played a key role in getting non-Indian support and negotiating peaceful resolutions to tense situations.
Courtesy: Museum of History & Industry

115

Bob Satiacum during one of his multiple appearances in court during the sixties and early seventies. Courtesy: The Post Intelligencer Collection. Museum of History & Industry

authorities on the Puyallup and Nisqually rivers. The goal of the two Indian organizations was to defend Indian rights as federal and state governments continually changed their policies in how to deal with the Indian problem.

The harassment against Indians had begun soon after Isaac Stevens was appointed governor and superintendant of Indian affairs. Initially the whites had charged that the Indians were not making proper use of the land. From that time on, the whites came up with various positions on how to deal with the issues that the Indians were demanding. In 1887, the federal government had passed the Dawes Act, which divided up Indian reservations into allotments to individual Indians who would hopefully become self-sufficient farmers. This did not happen because the tribes were not adept at farming. In truth they were too strongly tied to their traditional ways of providing sustenance to their families as fishermen. As a result of this law, the reservation lost more land and the Indians became more impoverished. In 1934, the federal government, under the focus of the New Deal, reversed itself when President Franklin Delano Roosevelt extended privileges of self-government and special benefits to the tribes. In 1953, federal policy reversed again as Congress passed Concurrent Resolution 108, which mandated a move towards "termination" of the special relationship between Native peoples and the federal government at the "earliest possible date." This was designed to remove any support Indians had always relied on from the federal government.

Confusing and inconsistent federal policy continued into the 1960s. In 1942, the court proposed a limited interpretation of native fishing rights in Tulee v. Washington granting its support for fishing rights by insisting that the treaty "leaves the state with power to impose on Indians equally with others as necessary for the conservation of fish."

In 1957, a split decision in State v. Satiacum was more definitive, ruling that the treaties "will continue to be superior to the exercise of the state's police power." Satiacum knew it would be important to continue fishing and try to turn his actions into legal cases. As time went on, he was caught fishing and he appeared in court multiple times trying to defend himself. In every case, he was unsuccessful because of biased judges and forceful prosecuting attorneys.

But in the 1963 Washington v. McCoy case, the court modified this principle and once again upheld the right of the state to subject Native Americans to "reasonable and necessary regulations." This confusing and contradictory background of precedent made it easy for judges in the early 1960s to simply pick and choose the decision that best supported their interpretations and dismiss the rest as irrelevant.

The press continued to present a negative image of Indians in the 1960s. In 1963, Walter Neubrech became the head enforcement for the Department of Game. *The Seattle Times*, in its April 20, 1962 article entitled "Skagits on the Warpath," presented an interview with Neubrech in which he made a number of charges that the Indians were becoming forceful in their behavior. He claimed that his officers were being shot at by the Indians. "They (the Indians) are crowding us," he stated.

In 1963 the state amended the laws based on Public Law 280 to extend civil jurisdiction without tribal consent over specified land and some specific activities on all reservations. Because of these actions the ACLU initiated its first involvement in favor of the Puyallup and Nisqually in their battle for Indian rights.

The overall methods of the Survival of the American Indian Association (SAIA) proved to be more successful than any previous attempts to resolve the fishing rights problem. The fish-ins and the involvement of the organizations listed above helped to move the Puyallup and Nisqually cause toward justice. The endorsements and help of churches headed by the Episcopal Bishop of the Diocese in Olympia helped to shift public opinion further. When U.S. Attorney Stanley Pitkin filed U.S. v. Washington, this case finally opened the way to a Federal Court hearing and trial in 1974.

After reviewing the problems and issues, attorneys representing both sides presented a case that was taken to court in 1973. United States District Court Judge Boldt was chosen to preside over the trial. He had no prior knowledge of Indian law but he was determined to examine both sides of this issue thoroughly, in order to reach a just settlement.

The Indians were pleased that, after so long a battle for their fishing rights, their case would finally be reviewed in a court of law. They were hopeful they might finally gain something of importance. They had been deprived of justice since the whites first came to their homeland; they were unsure of how the rulings would come. They remembered the stance that Judge Jacques of the Pierce County Superior Court took in stating "They never meant for you people to be free like everyone else." They also remembered when Harmon, the Pierce County assistant prosecutor said, "We had the power and force to exterminate these people from the face of the earth, instead of making treaties with them. Perhaps we should have. We certainly wouldn't be having all this trouble with them today."

On the other hand, the whites were nervous about the ruling, too. Since they first discovered the great salmon runs in both the Puyallup and Nisqually rivers in the 1800s, they had long thought that all the salmon was theirs for the taking. They had never understood the needs of the Indians or the legalities of the Medicine Creek Treaty of 1854. Since their numbers had grown, the whites felt no need to share the salmon with anyone.

The Medicine Creek (She-nah-nam) Treaty was a document of thirteen articles between the United States Government and the Puyallup, Nisqually, Steilacoom tribes, along with the Suawskin, S'Homamish, Stehchass, T'Peeksin, Squi-aitl, and Sa-heh-wamish tribes. The treaty granted 2.24 million acres of land to the United States in exchange for the establishment of three reservations, cash payments over a period of twenty years, and the recognition of traditional native fishing and hunting rights.

On February 12, 1974, Judge Boldt affirmed the Indians' right to fish in their accustomed places, as stated in the Medicine Creek Treaty of 1854. Courtesy: Sand Point Archives

Those rights had been ignored by the territorial and later the Washington State Government.

Judge Boldt studied every aspect of the Medicine Creek Treaty in preparation for the trial that began on August 27, 1973. He held court six days a week until the case was completed. Forty-nine experts and tribal members testified. During the proceedings, both the Indians and the whites attentively observed everything that went on in the court. Both sides knew that much depended on the trial's outcome. Both knew it would affect the economic welfare of each for years to come. Both sides relied on the treaty clause that read, "The right of taking fish at usual and accustomed grounds and stations is further secured to said Indians in common with all citizens of the territory."

During the following months, Judge Boldt presided over a highly complex trial with a law-and-order firmness. Outside of the courtroom, white picketers carried protest signs and hangings in effigy of Judge Boldt, Inside, lawyers debated the central question: Could the state of Washington regulate the fishing practices of Indians who had signed treaties with the US Government? But the underlying question was farther-reaching: To what extent could tribes, as separate nations within a nation, rule their own people and control their own destinies? This was the most important question.

The state interpreted the words "In common with all citizens" to mean that Indians, like all other residents of the state, must be subject to state control. The Indians argued the treaty entitled them to fish unimpeded at any of their "usual and accustomed places." It was obvious that the whites wanted to control all ways of living and survival of the local native minority. The Indians, on the other hand, simply wanted to live their lives as they always had without the interference of anyone.

Testifying at the trial were Billy Frank Jr. and his father, who told stories passed on to them by their fathers and grandfathers. They talked of the time before white people came and of the generations of Indians that went back to the beginning of time. It was obvious that the Indians case was strong and undeniable. For some of the whites who watched the proceedings, they began to see some of the truths offered by the Indians.

After exhaustive hearings and investigations, Judge Boldt would find that Indian fishermen had not wasted fish or harmed the runs of salmon. These charges by whites suggested Indians were flouting state conservation laws. The whites deemed these laws sensible and just. They felt threatened by Indians who would not abide and accept them. Ironically, it was the government's own documents, those that were pushed by Isaac Stevens in the mid 1800s, which were used to state the Indian's case.

On February 12, 1974, Judge Boldt handed down his 203- page decision.

He affirmed the rights of Washington's Indians to fish in their accustomed places. The ruling also allocated fifty percent of the annual catch to the treaty tribes. The Puyallup, the Nisqually, the Muckleshoot, and other tribes that depended on salmon in the state of Washington won a great victory that day. Not all of the Indians were surprised. Many had known all along that they were right. They knew that once the white man understood justice and the power of treaties, they would have to come around and accept the law as it was agreed upon more than a hundred years ago at the federal level.

After decades of conflict, Indians fighting for their fishing rights in western Washington had finally won an important victory. Boldt, relying on an 1828 edition of Webster's American Dictionary, interpreted "in common with" to mean the Indians were entitled to half the harvestable salmon

Roberto Maestas, director of El Centro de la Raza, Bernard and Billy Frank Jr. at one of their celebratory meetings after the Boldt Decision was reached. Courtesy: Lawney Reyes

running through their traditional waters. The tribes were assured the right to fish at "usual and accustomed grounds and stations" by federal treaties signed in 1854. The ruling surprised even a number of Indians who were up to now doubtful. Over the years they had always been the scapegoat. They were surprised that a court of law made up of white men would rule in their favor.

Bill Lowman wore a symbolic arrow in his hat during a demonstration by non-Indian fishermen. They made plans for further demonstrations to protest the Boldt Decision and cuts in fishing time. Courtesy: The Seattle Times

121

Years after the Boldt Decision was reached, there was still evidence of protesters as seen by this ship pulling into Friday Harbor. Courtesy: The Seattle Times, 1978

The decision was the culmination of years of the State of Washington's limitation of treaty fishing by the tribes, resulting in the United States suing Washington to force the state to comply with the treaties. Non-Native fishermen immediately met the judgment with shock and outrage, but the ruling has held since that time.

When thousands of Sportsmen read about the Boldt Decision the following morning, there was great mourning, then anger. It was as if the world of the white man had ended. After the Boldt ruling, fishing in Commencement Bay changed. The harassment of Indian fishermen disappeared. Nevertheless, there was a lot of grumbling. The whites avoided confronting the Indians and kept their distance from the mouth of the Puyallup River. The tugboats, which for months had cruised the river to destroy and damage Indian fishing nets, finally stopped. The Tacoma police no longer patrolled the Bay and river in their boats at night.

After the ruling in favor of the Indians, the non-Indian fishermen were outraged. Some went to the water armed, hoping for direct confrontation with the Indians. There was conflict on the water, but the Indians were not to be manhandled. They were now ready to fight for their rights. There were demonstrations by whites outside of Judge Boldt's court in Tacoma and U.S. marshals were brought in to enforce the ruling and maintain order.

Western Washington tribes had been assured the right to fish at "usual and accustomed grounds and stations" by federal treaties signed in 1854 and 1855. But during the next fifty years, Euro-American immigrants, armed with larger boats, modern technology, and the regulatory muscle of the state, gradually displaced them.

After decades of injustice, the judicial system had finally faced the truth and ruled in favor of the Indians. Everyone who was familiar with the Medicine Creek Treaty felt Judge Boldt had no choice based on the treaties of the past. Over the years, in the fight for these rights, Billy Frank Jr. had taken the lead for the Nisqually and Bob Satiacum and his brothers, the Puyallup. These stalwarts had fought for their rights alongside other brave members of both tribes for decades, under much pressure from the white Sportsmen and Washington State authorities. This small number of Indians continued to fish regardless of the harassment directed against them.

The night after the announcement of Judge Boldt's decision, Satiacum and his crew, along with many others celebrated quietly at the J&M tavern on Pacific Avenue. They drank into the night, toasting each other. When they learned that

Billy Frank Jr. was appointed the Chairman of the Northwest Indian Fisheries Commission in 1975, a position he held for thirty-nine years. This photo was taken at the exact spot where the Medicine Creek Treaty was signed. Courtesy: Northwest Indian Fisheries Commission

Judge Boldt had ordered the state to take action to limit fishing by non-Indians, they went to the Milwaukee tavern next door to celebrate a little more.

Throughout western Washington, where whites lived along the coast, there were demonstrations against the Boldt Decision. A large number of whites gathered at these places with hand-painted signs protesting the decision. A number of them showed Judge Boldt hanging in effigy. The angry whites knew they had lost an important battle on the water, but it did not change their attitudes toward Indians. In fact, they were angrier than ever. They still hoped that one day they would win this war and move the Indians from the bay once and for all.

There was continued violence after the Boldt Decision was made public; the US Government finally intervened. The government, on behalf of the tribes, filed suit against the State of Washington.

It would take years for the wounds to heal in the white community. In many households, they would never heal. Only a small number of whites could not see the validity of the Medicine Creek Treaty that stated Indians would retain their right to fish as they always had.

To the whites, this had no bearing on what was happening now. Many would believe that the demise of the salmon was totally the fault of the Indians. For years to come, the white fishermen would never forgive Judge Boldt. For most of the Sportsmen who fished on Commencement Bay, their reasons for being there were dampened. Many had a hard time finding adventure now that they could not legally harass the Indians on the Bay.

The amount of salmon taken by the Indians did not change. They only took what was needed to support the needs of their families. The only time they exceeded this was when they needed to sell salmon to get money to buy other necessities. The Puyallup and the Nisqually went about the methods of fishing as they always had. They would do this whether whites were present or not. Even during the times of white confrontation, the Indian's method of fishing for salmon went on as it always had. Their methods of survival were not greatly influenced by the presence of whites one way or the other.

Only Satiacum proceeded to catch more fish. He wanted to let the whites know that he could be greedy, also. He wanted them to know that he understood the value and power of money and one day he would be rich.

Satiacum was well aware that Judge Boldt had carefully studied the reading of the treaty negotiations to determine the meaning of "in common with." He understood that the judge had to conclude that the United States intended for there to be an equal sharing of the fish resources between the tribes and the settlers. Furthermore, Satiacum expected that Boldt would make the tribes co-managers of the state's fisheries. He was well aware that this is what Billy Frank Jr. wanted. Satiacum knew, without a doubt, that his Nisqually friend could manage the fisheries better than anyone connected to state government. He knew his friend understood more about the life and habits of salmon than any white who lived in the state. Satiacum also knew that Billy Frank Jr. was fully aware of how the whites treated the environment and why this affected all salmon runs.

With the drop of a gavel, tribes were transformed, in the eyes of the law, from underground poaching societies to at-the-table equals with the state authorities that had persecuted them for so long.

The whites had to accept that the Indians certainly understood the law and the treaties that controlled them. Before that, they didn't think the Indians were intelligent enough to understand the clever and deceiving wording invented by the Federal Government to deal with Indian issues.

Judge Boldt's ruling revolutionized the state fishing industry. In 1975, Billy Frank Jr. was appointed the Chairman of the Northwest Indian Fisheries Commission; he held this position for almost forty years. In 1979, the Ninth Circuit Court of Appeals upheld Boldt's ruling and on July 2, 1979, the US Supreme Court affirmed it.

But what most observers didn't know was that the Boldt Decision brought responsible salmon management to the State of Washington. Before Boldt, the state didn't really know what salmon management was. After Boldt, for the first time, harvest quotas had to be clearly defined. Salmon began to be managed on a river-by-river basis. The shallow approach to salmon management by the whites was now gone.

This was an important victory not only for western Washington tribes but psychologically for all Indians in the nation. It showed that at least some whites had the capacity to be fair and function within the law. These victories lent a positive note for Indians all over the country. It provided unique challenges for many. For the first time in a long run, Indians were looked upon with some respect. Those people who had a small degree of Indian blood in their makeup, but who had hidden it in the past, now came forth to admit they were indeed part Indian. It soon became the "in thing," and the Red power movement throughout the country grew even stronger. The Boldt Decision has been used to define Indian and fishing rights' cases across the country, as well as to determine aboriginal rights as far away as Australia.

After the days of fierce conflict, Judge Boldt's health began to deteriorate. Surgery to repair an aortic aneurysm left him a changed man. On March 18, 1984, at the Veterans Administration Hospital in Tacoma, Judge Boldt died. The judge did not favor any one side in his interpretation of the law. All of his time on the bench, he deliberately stuck to the books in all of his rulings. Although he was acutely aware of the dismal and treacherous treatment of Indians by whites over the years, he did not let this influence his findings in a court of law.

After his death, his son stated in his eulogy. "He loved the law. He would not do anything to violate his duties as a judge."

9. Another Path

THE PREJUDICE OF THE WHITES against Indians still exists today in the Tacoma area. Some of it remains in the mindsets of whites who live near the Nisqually Reservation, at Frank's Landing. But because of shifting opinions, it is certainly less today. There is no question that many of the Sportsmen, and others of their kind, still harbor negative thoughts deep within themselves. These offspring of forebears from another land still cannot accept that others lived and developed unique and impressive cultures in the area long before they came.

Many of the Indians who went through the hard days of prejudice during the 40s, 50s, 60s and 70s, still remember the humiliation and hurt they experienced when white people came to claim the land, the water, the salmon and the Indians' rights. Those days are very hard to forget, especially for those who were young at the time. It was very difficult to be jobless and hungry and to be continually looked down upon, and to be without enough money to buy the necessities one needed from day to day. All were embarrassed to wear clothing that wasn't much more than rags or ill-fitting shoes that should have been discarded long before. It was degrading to endure the taunts of whites who wanted Indians to know they were nothing more than second-class citizens, if citizens at all.

However, this changed in 1924 when the Senate and House finally acknowledged that Indians should be allowed citizenry in the United States. Indian servicemen, on the battlefields in Europe, forced this into consideration after their courageous performances during World War I.

Those who have studied the past can readily testify that the United States history books have simply minimized or excluded the Indian's existence in their own country. For those Indians, who were fortunate enough to attend school and study the history of this country, it soon became apparent that they could not learn anything positive about their culture or appreciate any of the accomplishments of their people by reading US history books.

From the beginning, Hollywood movies portrayed Indians in a negative light. They were shown as ignorant savages or crafty killers standing in the way of the white man's progress. When the movies focused on the cowboy and Indian genre the results became humorous and predictable as Indians, on horseback, circled the wagon trains of whites until the last warrior was shot from the horse he rode. The Indians became nothing more than body counts, unable to cope with the firepower of the valiant white man defending the rights of his family and his kind.

One might question, why did it happen? Why had authors of books and literature and producers and directors of moving pictures treat Indians in this manner? What had the Indians done to deserve this? This observer has to conclude that it was a cover up, spawned by guilt. Thinking whites must have known of the crimes committed by their own, as they came by the thousands to kill, take possession of the land and finally pollute everything in sight. They must have sensed the conspiracy. Many certainly wanted to hide it. They didn't want anyone to know that they were related or descended from such conniving forebears.

To conceal these crimes to those living and to others who would come in the future, something had to be done to prevent them from knowing what really happened. The best solution would be to make the Indians invisible in their own land. The best way to do this was to exclude them from history books and literature in general; to defame them in movies as something less than civilized seemed another way to go. This was easily done because the authors of books and the producers and directors of movies were, for the most part, white.

Observers would later compare this to the atrocities of book burning by the Nazis prior to World War II. The Nazis burned books to prevent the sharing of knowledge or the understanding of truth, whereas white America conveniently excluded natives by not writing about them. This would eventually prevent Indians from being a part of history in their own land; their great leaders, heroes and their accomplishments would never be recognized.

In 1964, with the appearance of Marlon Brando, some attitudes of the dominant culture in Tacoma began to change. The support Brando gave to Indians fighting for their fishing rights had some effect on the white population but it was felt deeply and appreciated by all Indians. The Puyallup and the Nisqually were pleased to see at least one white was on their side. They were pleased that someone of Brando's stature would stand and speak up on their behalf. It gave them some confidence to know they were not in this fight alone. For the first time, a few whites who agreed with Brando could now see that the Indian fishermen had a case.

Dick Gregory, a world famous comedian at this time, had joined the cause of the Indian fishermen in February of 1966; he proudly accepted the invitation to join them on the Nisqually River. Like Brando, he faced a degree of opposition; he and his wife were chastised continually. Gregory spent nearly six months in prison on charges of illegal net fishing. He chose to remain in jail, even when the possibility of release was offered. Gregory liked the idea of publicizing what he claimed was one of the most important "civil-rights" fights going on in the nation at the time.

The positive achievements since Marlon Brando and Dick Gregory's visit had opened the eyes of both whites and Indians. The whites realized now that they might have underestimated the ability of Indians. Some probably admitted the redskins were smarter than they once thought.

Many began to understand that the shortage of salmon was not the fault of the Indian fishermen. Some now agreed that commercial ocean fishers had a strong impact on the number of salmon that entered the Bay. Others became aware the logging companies that cut trees indiscriminately in the forests had destroyed important spawning grounds.

A few sensed that pollution by large corporations and people in general was sickening and probably killing much of the salmon population. Based

Dick Gregory was arrested and spent almost six months in jail for participating in
Nisqually fish-ins. He willingly accepted this sentence because he knew it was for
a good cause. This photo was taken on the steps of the courthouse. Courtesy: The
Post-Intelligencer Collection, Museum of History & Industry

on the amount of pollution in the country, in particular the water, it's a
wonder that there are any salmon left at all.

During those times the Indians in the area must have felt that every
white person in Tacoma was against them. But in truth most whites did not
think of Indians one way or another. They were too busy trying to eke out a
living for themselves and their families, from day to day.

In the upper parts of Tacoma and on Broadway where whites who were
well off lived and congregated, Indians were never seen. If anyone wanted
to see Indians, they could only be found on one block along lower Pacific
Avenue, between 13th and 14th streets. To get a closer look, one would have
to enter the three taverns; the Anchor, the Milwaukee, and the J&M. The
only other places where Indians could be found were in the poorer sections
of the Portland Avenue area near Salishan or certain parts of the Fife to the
east where rents were cheap. No self-respecting white person would ever be
found there.

If whites became aware of Indian problems in the area, they read about
them in articles in the local newspapers. If they learned that Indians were

destroying the salmon runs, it came from gossip by the Sportsmen or those who supported the whites out on the water.

Closer observation found that those who opposed Indians were simply whites who were engaged in the salmon-fishing controversy. They were in large numbers and they were determined to make things right as they saw it by suppressing the Indians' methods of catching salmon, not only how they fished but where they fished.

Although a large number of whites in Tacoma looked down upon Indians, there were others who thought differently. These were people who were fair minded and trying to live their lives privately, in a good way. They were simply law-abiding citizens who had no quarrel with anyone.

There were those who could recognize injustice, especially when it was directed against others. These people would direct their energies to making things right. Two such people were Reverend Robert Johnson and Dorothy Creevy. Robert Johnson was the pastor for the Presbyterian Church near Portland Avenue. Dorothy Creevy played the organ at the church and wanted everyone to have a good time while together on Sundays. Both were aware how Indians were treated in Tacoma and they did what they could to relieve the fears and tensions these people experienced. Most of their congregation was made of Indians with a smaller number of whites. On Sunday, when everyone gathered, it was a friendly and heart-warming place to be.

Reverend Johnson and Mrs. Creevy were kind and generous people who believed in God and fair play, and every Sunday they tried to share their beliefs and good will with everyone who attended the services.

In time the feelings against Indians would change. With the continued fish-ins and protests by a larger number of Indians and supportive non-Indians, the overall population of whites began to take notice. Newspaper articles supporting the Indian's cause from other cities and states began to form favorable opinions.

In 1990, Dances with Wolves, one of the first movies to emerge from Hollywood in a long time with strong positive notes about Indians and their culture, was shown to large audiences all over the country. It was well received, especially by Indians. The movie was a real and accurate education for most whites. Later, it won the Oscar for best picture of the year. This movie and another like it Broken Arrow , that had come decades earlier, with James Stewart and Jeff Chandler as Cochise, offered the nation a new perspective of American Indians. A large number of people in the United States viewed the first picture thoughtfully and learned much about the Plains Indians and their way of living and thinking. This, in turn, moved many white people to reconsider their age-old thoughts of all Indians as being nothing more than savages and obstructions to progress.

In 2002, the National Museum of the American Indian in Washington DC was opened to overflowing crowds. To ensure that the museum represented the thought and desires of all Indians, a number of representatives throughout the nation were called in to share their thoughts, to form an overall philosophy. Bernie Whitebear, Vine Deloria, and other respected Indians across the country, under the direction of Rick West, the director, were invited to sit on the board of regents.

On the opening day of the museum, it seemed that every Indian in the United States was there to celebrate. The beautiful building sits on the last six acres of the Smithsonian complex and provides a welcome counterpart to the East-wing Museum of Modern Art.

The museum offers the viewing public an opportunity to study about a million artifacts of the many tribes who lived throughout the North-American continent. This magnificent display began to cause whites to think differently about American Indian art and artifacts. Once, the creations of Indians were considered inferior to art created by whites. In a number of cases the art and creations of Indians were burned by whites who could not recognize the value of the work. Now the art is being evaluated in a more open manner. It is looked upon by many as a national treasure.

All of the above accomplishments in favor of Indians have somewhat changed the attitudes of both Indians and whites. It has given Indians a positive outlook that did not exist for over a hundred years. Many young Indians can now see the advantage of trying to make it in the mainstream. Many have gone on to schools of higher learning. A number have reached out to the professional fields of engineering, medicine, and law. The very young are now receiving promising guidance in their head-start programs that make them happy to be Indian. The elders are finally receiving the healthcare and respect that was withheld from them for over a century.

All of this is much different than the days prior to the late 1800s when it was the attitude of most whites in the United States that all Indians should be exterminated. The only thing that prevented this from happening was the belief of one man, Colonel Pratt, who suggested to Congress that what needed killing was the Indian beliefs and religion. Off Reservation Indian Boarding Schools were established in the country, the first being Carlisle in Pennsylvania and the second Chemawa in Oregon. Others soon appeared in other parts of the country. The schools were purposely placed far from the reservations where the young Indians lived. Those in charge at the schools wanted to enforce rules that would permanently erase family ties or any other ties the young had to their culture.

The young usually came from broken homes and were transported to the schools where the process of stripping them from their cultures began. In the beginning this was done forcibly not allowing the young to use their native language or practicing anything akin to their culture. The idea was to destroy the Indian beliefs and culture that all the young Indians had been taught earlier. At times, the young Indians were treated harshly and whipped and beaten to make them conform. The schools made sure that the young came from different tribes. They wanted to make sure that everyone would have a hard time relating to one another.

There were times when the young Indians became sick and died, never to return to their homelands. In most cases there was no money to pay for their transport. Afterwards generations of young Indians were affected by this treatment. Later, it became difficult to find any young Indian who was completely in tune with the teachings of their elders or the traditions of their tribes.

Some whites feel they should honor and be proud of what Indian blood flows through their veins. Other whites will admit, with reservations, that they have Indian blood in their make-up because they suspect there might be some money in it. After all, isn't this the American way of weighing things?

Regardless how one looks at it, the attitudes noted are real. There is hope that some Indians will benefit from the changed attitudes. It has been proven in times past that when there is hope and consideration, all kinds of good things can come of it.

Others felt it would be good to be associated by blood with such great Indian athletes as Jim Thorpe, Alex Arcasa, Sockalexis, Roberto Duran, Billy

Mills, and Brett Favre. Many whites who sought entertainment in other areas such as the theater were impressed with the beautiful and expressive movements of the highest-paid ballet dancer in the world, Maria Tallchief, who was the first prima ballerina in the United States.

In the field of music and film, several would be surprised to know that great singers such as Kay Starr, Lee Wiley, and Keely Smith were part Indian. In film, it became noteworthy to include great actors such as Robert Mitchum, Val Kilmer, Wes Studi, Linda Darnell, Ava Gardner, Ann Miller and one of the greatest entertainers of all time, Elvis Presley.

Decades of continued abuse had a detrimental but far-reaching effect on Satiacum, his brothers Buddy and Junior, and a number of others in the Puyallup tribe. The long years of harassment toughened them, and they would never be able to face or accept anyone at face value if they were not Indian. If the non-Indians were white, there would always be an aura of suspicion. It is certain these feelings and attitudes would last a lifetime.

Billy Frank Jr. and the Bridges family of the Nisqually, surviving as best they could on their small reservation, had suffered even longer. Whether they liked it or not, they would harbor the same feelings as the Puyallup.

A small number of Indians of other tribes, who were willing to fight for Indian rights on the waters of the Puyallup and the Nisqually rivers, such as Hank Adams, The Quinault, Bernard Reyes, Su'Zan Satiacum, and Don and Janet McCloud continually shared in the abuse of the white authorities. Although they were not native to the rivers, they felt it was their responsibility to support their friends regardless of the odds.

They probably never realized their efforts and determination would finally end in a most important victory in 1974, with the Boldt decision. They would certainly be surprised to know their accomplishments would affect the mindsets of all Indians and a number of non-Indians across the nation.

There were never any level playing fields for Indians in those early days. But now some things had changed for what some consider the good, and these stalwarts mentioned above are now recognized for their efforts. People today who understand and appreciate what they stood for and accomplished view them with a great measure of respect.

After fishing with Bob Satiacum for seven years, Bernard had returned his net, his canoe, and his Mercury motor to his friend's backyard. He decided

After moving to Seattle, Bernard spent the rest of his life fighting for Indian rights. He was invited to sit on the board of regents for the National Museum of the American Indians in Washington, DC. Courtesy: Lawney Reyes

to devote his time to helping Indians of all tribes who were moving into Seattle. Bernard was aware that many Indians were moving in from different parts of the country. He thought it important to help those who were down and out to adjust to urban living. He knew many Indians who had spent their entire lives living on an Indian reservation would need help and direction in adjusting to a new way of life.

Bernard believed that it would be important to set up a healthcare system to tend to the needs of hundreds of Indians moving into the city, Indians who could not afford proper healthcare.

Bernard also knew that Indians who were persuaded to move to cities would eventually need a land base that they could relate to; this would be his most important goal. He had become known at this time in Seattle as Bernie Whitebear. It was a name he had chosen to honor his grandfather, White Grizzly Bear, who was well known in Castlegar, British Columbia. His grandfather was a great hunter and guide and was respected for years in the British Columbia area by many whites before he and his family were forcibly displaced by others from Russia who had moved into their beloved homeland where the Kootenay and Columbia rivers join.

During the late fall of 1974, Satiacum felt regret as he watched The Quinault load his canoe, net, and gear onto his pick-up. His dear friend had fished with him for over eighteen years and he suspected this season might be his last. Now that the war with the whites was won, the man from Taholah could see no reason for returning to Tacoma. He wanted to return to the quiet atmosphere of his homeland, along the banks of the Quinault River, void of any white men.

Satiacum appreciated the fact that his friend from Taholah was an able man always near to support him over the years. He could not think of anyone who could fish better or help him more on the water during those trying times. He smiled when be observed that only a few in the Tacoma area knew his real name, Clifford Mowich. He had always been referred to by most as The Quinault.

Before his friend from Taholah drove away, Satiacum voiced "You're going to miss Chester's cooking. Remember there are no Chinese restaurants where you live and there is no one in the world who can cook as well as Chester."

After those exciting times, action on the water changed. The Puyallup fished in their accustomed manner, taking only enough salmon to feed their families and use as trade for other goods with the Yakima. They fished during the day and no longer feared harassment from white authorities. The whites continued to fish in great numbers on Commencement Bay, sticking with their own and ignoring the Indians. Now activity on the water seemed almost dull for the Sportsmen, who had used unbridled methods of harassing and mistreating Indians for decades.

Bob Satiacum, who suffered first-hand abuse and harassment of whites for many years, was pleased with the outcome. But he vowed to continue the fight against the unjust practices of the whites. He was determined to make the whites pay for their unfair treatment of Indians and make as much money as he could to right old wounds. No one in his tribe faced the hardships and prejudice longer than he had. During his long fight against white intolerance, his courage was unmatched. Many times he fought the battles single-handedly. He was always outnumbered, but he never gave in to the biased and continuing affronts of the whites.

After the Boldt decision, Satiacum left the fishing of salmon to his brothers. He decided to direct his efforts to making money. He hired others to fish for him and in addition to the sale of salmon, he began to make money in the sale of tax-free cigarettes. Satiacum soon found that this was an easy way of making money. All he had to do was hire someone to build a small stand to house the business and then hire another to manage it. Indian Bob liked this type of business because it did not interfere with his principle business of salmon sales. But his success in the ventures of fishing and cigarettes encouraged him to think of other ways of making even more money. He wanted to let everyone know he could involve himself in successful businesses never before considered by an Indian.

Later, he devoted much time in finding a way to sell tax-free alcohol. He figured if he could sell the hard stuff and not charge sales tax, he could make a bundle. The thought of going into competition with the Washington State Liquor stores amused him. He knew the principle difficulties of such a business would be in finding the sources that he could depend on.

Satiacum seemed driven to make as much money as he could. This is where he differed from Billy Frank Jr., Bernie Whitebear, and The Quinault. These three friends of his were more interested in Indian rights and sustaining the traditional way of life for their people. They would forego moneymaking schemes and devote their lives to what they thought was best for their people, to regain some of the ways of life that had been taken from them.

Bob did understand the problems his tribe faced and was willing to help his people out in any way he could, but he felt that he must improve his own lot in life. It is true that he wanted to get even with the whites for what they had done to his people for decades. Satiacum was painfully aware of the poverty his tribe had long faced because of the whites; he wanted the whites to pay.

With one successful endeavor after another, he found that everything he turned to seemed to work. He could measure all this by the amount of money he made. Satiacum never forgot Philip Martin and what he had learned from him as a young man. He remembered how he had brought his tribe out of abject poverty. Satiacum hoped that he might be able to help his people in the same manner.

During the following years, he continued to amass a fortune. Bob Satiacum's life was becoming one big party after another. He drank hard, but never once had anyone been in his company when he was intoxicated. He dined at the best restaurants and tipped well.

Most whites did not like him, but bartenders and barmaids always welcomed his presence because of the amount of money he spent and the tips he left. He was well disciplined and always in control. Although he spent a lot of time in taverns and cocktail lounges with friends he never smoked or used foul language. No one could remember him saying anything derogatory about anyone. There was always humor and he seemed to like everyone. But Satiacum was showing, for all to see, that money could buy anything. He was simply having a good time and living life to the fullest.

During this time rumors were circulating that he was hooking up with the Mafia. Someone had seen him meeting with individuals connected with the mob; others thought they might have come from New York City to meet with Bob. Although law enforcement officials in Olympia and Tacoma were keeping an eye on him, Satiacum's connection to the Mafia could never be substantiated.

It was at this time that Satiacum conceived of the idea of creating a nightclub. He thought this would be the first time such a business was ever opened and owned by an Indian. He felt a fitting title for his new venture would be "Bob Satiacum's Place."

On opening night his nightclub was an immediate success. Both the Indians and the whites were surprised to see this happen. There was standing room only that night as a multitude of customers came, both Indians and whites. Satiacum could see that a number of the whites who came were the Sportsmen who had harassed him on the water of Commencement Bay. He didn't mind as long as they spent money to fill his coffers and pay his bills.

Satiacum was amused at the behavior of the whites. He knew they were there to see if his newborn business would be a success. He knew that whites were a curious lot who could not resist the temptation to learn anything new when it came to Indians. It seemed to him that they were always exploring and studying the behavior of Indians, much like anthropologists.

He hoped they would enjoy themselves and pass the word among friends about the great new club on Portland Avenue that was owned by an Indian. Satiacum could not have been more pleased with his success. After the first night of business, he had become a celebrity. As the cash registers filled, Indian Bob was already thinking of other ventures where he could make even more money.

While Billy Frank Jr. was fulfilling his quest of preservation of the environment and teaching the state of Washington how Indians had always cared for salmon, Satiacum was now seen all over town. He could be found in the best restaurants, expensive clothiers, best cocktail lounges, and the most exclusive auto dealers. It was irritating for the white Sportsmen to see him driving his expensive cars. He now owned a long list of the best: a custom made black Lincoln Continental with an expensive black leather interior, a Pontiac Firebird, an Austin-Healey sports car. He enjoyed driving them in the countryside, east of Puyallup, usually breaking the speed limit. Satiacum was purposely flaunting his newfound wealth. Later, his brother, Buddy, bought him an elegant Rolls Royce, which he happily added to his collection. This really antagonized his critics.

Afterwards, Satiacum purchased a very large, expensive boat that measured over twenty-eight feet. From that point on he could be seen maneuvering his luxurious vessel, with a number of Indian friends aboard toasting each other with expensive bottles of champagne that he always had on board. Sometimes, he would take the boat to Seattle and ride about Lake Union and through the Crittendon Locks to reach the Sound. It was obvious to everyone that he was having the time of his life, displaying and spending his wealth.

On one occasion, when traveling through the Seattle Locks, Satiacum encountered several dozen boats waiting in a long line to get through. Instead of waiting his turn, he drove to the front of the line and muscled his way in. Because of the size of his boat, he had no trouble doing this. It angered every white person in line and they shouted obscenities. Satiacum appreciated the fact that the angry whites had to look up at him, since they were in smaller boats and closer to the water. He merely smiled good-naturedly, waved, and invited everyone over to his boat for a drink of the finest liquor money could buy. He never had any takers.

Later, Satiacum reserved a jet at the Seattle-Tacoma International Airport to transport his entire family, and several relatives and friends, to Hawaii. Everyone in the party enjoyed themselves for an entire week at his expense. He had been poor most of his life and now that he could afford anything he wanted, he loved sharing what he had with others who were not as fortunate. Although this was greatly appreciated by relatives and friends in the Puyallup tribe, this did not set well with whites who, in the past, had always mistreated Indians in the Tacoma area. They resented Satiacum's success and the wealth he had accumulated. They felt he was flaunting it simply to irritate them; they were right.

"Indian Bob" had lived in the meanest of shelters all of his life, as did everyone in the tribe. Like all tribal members, they couldn't afford anything better. Now that he could afford it, he decided to purchase a grand old house along I-5 in the Fife area. Although it was built in an earlier period, it was in perfect shape and had a feeling of elegance. Later, he built a large structure alongside his house with a sliding roof to house a swimming pool. This gave him a degree of privacy and quiet from the noise generated from auto traffic along the I-5 freeway. He enjoyed sitting alongside the pool and having drinks with friends while watching every Indian kid in the neighborhood having the time of their life.

Satiacum knew his methods of accomplishing things might seem bizarre to others but he found them to his liking. He could not resist. This was his way of getting even with those who had oppressed his people for years and made life difficult. It was like a game to him. A game he thoroughly enjoyed.

No one would ever know the amount of money Satiacum accumulated during his rags to riches adventure in life. Time would pass before anyone would ever know the influence Satiacum would have on younger Indians who were still, in other ways, fighting for their rights.

Now, Su'Zan happily spent her time at their gracious home, being a housewife and mother. These good times continued until the day Satiacum was charged with tax evasion and ordered to appear before a court of law.

From the beginning, Su'Zan suspected that Satiacum did not have a chance to win. She could see that evidence had been accumulating against him and the law was determined to convict him.

Satiacum was aware the state authorities were after him. For years, the State of Washington considered him a thorn in their side. It had started with the fishing issue. Next, it was the selling of tax-free cigarettes; then problems arose with the distribution of fireworks. He seemed to be one step ahead of the state at every turn. He suspected that eventually they would try to get him on the non-payment of taxes.

After enduring Bob Satiacum's success for the last few years, his enemies in Tacoma and Olympia finally saw that his good times were threatened. Adversaries of the Puyallup were certain that the state would catch up with him soon. He had run rough shod over the authorities ever since the Boldt Decision and he was contemptuous of the state. He had made many enemies over the years, including some jealous members in his own tribe. Now those factions were pleased that the state was making headway and would one day have enough evidence to put him away.

Eventually, the state gathered the evidence they needed. They investigated and confirmed they could indeed get him on non-payment of taxes. After a hearing in Seattle, Satiacum was indicted. He had hired an attorney in Seattle, Wes Holbein, to fight his case but the attorney failed to come up with a good defense. Holbein seemed more interested in having his picture taken alongside his client than defending him in a court of law. Satiacum could not get any effective witnesses to help him. Actually, no one knew enough about his business dealings to be of any importance. Any testimony presented by his friends proved they would not stand up in a court of law.

One day, he disappeared. The authorities were completely baffled and had no clue to his whereabouts. It became a big mystery not only to whites, but to most Indians, as well. Everyone was aware he had amassed a fortune but no one knew where he or his money might be. As months turned to years, many began to forget about him and their interest turned to other things.

Years later, Satiacum made a simple, but costly, mistake. He telephoned relatives in Tacoma from a town in British Columbia where he had been hiding. The Northwest Mounted Police traced the call. To their embarrassment, they found his place of residence was only a few locks from their headquarters.

The Mounties, who always get their man, quickly surrounded the small house where Satiacum lived. They could not believe that he had resided, for nearly five years, within a stone's throw from their offices. When they angrily crashed through the door, they found him calmly sitting in a lounge chair enjoying a beer and watching television with two British Columbia Indians. He greeted them with a grin, "What kept you guys? Anyone want a beer?"

Satiacum was transferred to a prison in Vancouver BC. The charge was tax evasion. During this time many visitors came. While he was in seclusion, he had made many friends in the Indian communities of British Columbia.

Often, they would bring dried smoked salmon and baked salmon eggs, which the Puyallup relished.

One day in 1985 Bernie Whitebear drove to Vancouver BC with his brother to support his friend. He wanted to speak on behalf of Satiacum at the hearing. Whitebear had become an expert speaker and did an eloquent job of presenting a defense. He told about all that his friend had accomplished for decades as he fought for Indian fishing rights in the state of Washington; spoke of how he had supported others in his tribe, always out of his own pocket. But the judicial system in Vancouver BC was not impressed. However, the Canadian Indians that were present in the courtroom noted Whitebear's ability to express himself. In time, they learned to declare their own rights and fight for justice in British Columbia, using the Seattle Indian's methods.

As time passed, Satiacum began getting thinner and his complexion paled. He looked soft. This was due to his imprisonment and lack of exercise. He became resigned to being in prison and had no hope of ever getting out. But his spirits were always up and he enjoyed the visits of friends from Seattle and Tacoma. The old familiar Satiacum laugh always greeted them. Everyone could tell that he was never a man to feel sorry for himself.

Many Sportsmen in the state of Washington received the news of Satiacum's imprisonment with a great deal of satisfaction. At many taverns and bars in the Tacoma area they toasted each other and relished the fact that they had won an important victory, a victory that had been a long time in coming. But for all of them, it was worth the wait.

During Satiacum's imprisonment both Indians and whites kept track of his handling of the situation. They knew he would take it hard being placed behind bars. The whites feared that he would one day be released and they would again be faced with his arrogant way of doing business and making big money again. They hoped he would die in prison. On the other hand, most Indians hoped the courts would be lenient and set him free. Despite his imprisonment, family and friends carried on his business dealings in the Tacoma area and continued to make money.

In the early spring of 1991, 'Indian Bob' made the front page in *The Seattle Times* and the *Seattle Post Intelligencer* once again. The media had a field day when they reported that Satiacum, at the age of sixty-two, died of a stroke. But every Indian knew better. They knew he died because he was no longer free. Nearly everyone in Tacoma, white and Indian, was affected by his death. If anyone in the area was unaware of who Bob Satiacum was, they knew now because of the extensive coverage by the newspapers and television channels.

Close friends were not surprised when they heard the news of Satiacum's death. They were aware that he was having a difficult time in the Vancouver prison. All Indians accepted that Satiacum was a warrior and was put on this earth to be free. Like other great Indians of the past, who were imprisoned by the white man, they either committed suicide or willed themselves to die.

All knew that Indians were not unlike other animals of the land that needed to be free. They were not designed by the Great Power to be caged and put behind bars. Most were proud to be a friend of this great man. Almost all knew he was one of the most important forces the Indians had in the fight for Indian fishing rights in Western Washington. Many felt that Bob Satiacum and Billy Frank Jr.'s efforts would never be matched.

On March 30th, 1991, a huge memorial was held on the lawns of Cushman Indian Hospital. Over three thousand people attended. Many in the crowd, both white and Indian, were enemies of Satiacum but out of curiosity or

Bernard (Bernie Whitebear) and Allison Bridges remained friends for many years after the Last Fish War. Courtesy: Lawney Reyes

After the Boldt Decision, Bob Satiacum went on to amass a fortune in his rags to riches journey. Courtesy: The Post Intelligencer Collection, Museum of History & Industry

spite, they were there. A group of singers and drummers had come from the Yakima Indian Reservation in eastern Washington to pay tribute to Satiacum. Everyone was held spellbound by the beauty of their singing and their contribution to the service.

Dozens of friends and volunteers took turns carrying his casket to its final resting place high upon a hill overlooking his beloved Puyallup River. There were representatives from many tribes quietly paying homage. For those who were there, it was a beautiful spectacle to see. Bob Satiacum had never been paid so much respect until 'he came home in a casket' as the Seattle Times printed it, solemnly covering the event.

Nine years later on July 16th 2000, Bernie Whitebear passed away in Seattle. A number of celebrations were held to honor his achievements in life before his death. Everyone remembered that he was the first Indian to get land returned for Indian use only. The City of Seattle granted Bernie's organization, the United Indians of All Tribes Foundation, twenty acres of land to build his Daybreak Star Center. The lease was for ninety-nine years.

Many activities took place at the center during the thirty years of his leadership. Both Indians and whites used the facilities for a number of purposes. More than once politicians such as Governor Mike Lowry and

Mayors Charles Royer and Paul Schell threw fund raising events at the center to raise money for their campaigns. Mountaineers such as Jim Whittaker and James Wickwire and a large number in their organization used the center to raise funds for their expeditions. Close to a hundred and fifty marriages took place there. What events most pleasing to many were the Dinner Theaters where young Indians modeled traditional attire while large numbers consumed Indian prepared salmon and other traditional foods favored by Indians. At the end of July of every year, a large pow-wow was held to coincide with Sea-Fair Days in Seattle where many tribes came to perform, compete for prizes and simply enjoy each other's company.

After Bernie's death on July 21st a squad of sixteen motorcycle patrolmen accompanied by eight Muckleshoot friends on large Harley-Davidsons led the way to his memorial in the Convention Center in downtown Seattle. Dozens of family and friends followed in a long line of cars with their headlights on. Over two thousand friends and admirers assembled at the center including a number of tribal leaders, two senators, Daniel Inouye and Patty Murray, two governors, Mike Lowry and Gary Locke, mayor, Paul Schell, a county executive, Ron Sims and a Washington State representative Jay Inslee who later became the governor of Washington State.

Daniel Inouye, the senator from Hawaii and a personal friend of Bernie, flew in to attend the memorial. He was greeted with a standing ovation by the large crowd. Senator Inouye then walked to the podium and presented a moving eulogy. He ended his talk by stating; "Bernie Whitebear was a great leader. He was known and admired all the way from the state of Washington to the city of Washington." Afterwards, Governor Gary Locke walked to the podium and shared his thoughts. "In 1997 I declared that Bernie Whitebear was the Citizen of the Decade in the state of Washington. I erred, he is truly the Citizen of the Century." The memorial ended when singers and drummers of the Nez Perce performed the beautiful "Old Warriors Song."

In Seattle, not long after his death, a Jewish committee headed by Peter and Hinda Schnurman had seven trees planted in Israel to honor Bernie's achievements in life.

Following Judge Boldt's decision, Billy Frank Jr. devoted the rest of his life to the preservation of salmon and the environment. He worked day and night to teach unsympathetic white legislators at the state capitol in Olympia how

145

to preserve the salmon that came from the ocean into the rivers he loved. During his leadership the National Indian Fisheries Commission, based in Olympia, Washington, would grow to have satellite offices in Forks and Mount Vernon. It grew to staff sixty-five people in an effort to educate the uninformed on subjects ranging from fish health to salmon management planning and habitat protection.

Billy was always in demand to speak about this subject matter at numerous conventions. He was never interested in making money for himself but he wanted to share his knowledge of the salmon and the environment, a subject he knew better than anyone in the state of Washington. Soon Billy Frank Jr. would be acknowledged a real hero by all Indians and others in the state and beyond. He overcame personal tragedies to help save a precious resource, not only for his people, but for the broader society that was heedlessly ignoring and destroying it.

Later, the man from Nisqually was awarded the Albert Schweitzer Prize for Humanitarianism, joining past winners: former President Jimmy Carter and former U.S. Surgeon General Dr. C. Everett Koop.

On May 5, 2014, Billy Frank Jr. died unexpectedly at his family home near the Nisqually river. He had just taken a shower and dressed for an appointment when his son found him on his bed, slumped over. In spite of his beatings, his times in jail, the lies hurled at him by deceitful whites and the numerous battles he lost against the State of Washington, he had finally won his war.

Many tribal dignitaries came to his funeral along with the Governor, Jay Inslee, the Washington State Senator, Maria Cantwell and other important public servants. Over six thousand people attended while a large number watched the proceedings on large TV screens. To put it simply, it was a solemn but wonderful event for a hero, a giant among men.

Recognizing Billy Frank Jr's efforts and achievements, Governor Jay Inslee called him not just a tribal leader but a state leader. "We can't overstate how long lasting his legacy will be. He pushed the state when it needed to be pushed. He reminded the state when it needed reminding. His legacy is going to be with us for generations. My grandkids are going to benefit from his work."

Another accolade was presented from "America has lost a giant" by

Billy Frank Jr., who led Northwest tribes fighting for their treaty fishing rights, died at the age of 83. During his lifetime, he was awarded the Albert Sweitzer Award for Humanitarianism, an award he truly earned. Courtesy: Ann Yow/The Seattle Times file, 1983

Jeff Shaw, NC Policy Watch. "If you care about the U.S. Constitution, you should care about Billy Frank Jr. If you're concerned with honoring oaths and the dignity of keeping your word, you should be glad he lived. If you fight for social justice in any capacity, you had a fellow traveler. If you're concerned about the fate of the planet we're leaving to our children, you owe him a debt."

On November 18, 2015, Billy Frank Jr. the humble man from Nisqually, received the nation's highest civilian award, the Presidential Medal of Freedom.

It would be years before anyone would realize the impact Bob Satiacum, Billy Frank. Jr. and a small number of allies had on the battle for Indian fishing rights in the state of Washington. To this day, few would remember what they went through and how long they fought against untold numbers of whites and the power they wielded.

Today, any observer would be hard put to find anyone anywhere who could match the courage and determination of this small number of Washington State Indians. It is hard to imagine the energy and drive these stalwarts had in coping against incredible odds with those who were intent on destroying their well being and their way of life. From the beginning, the cards were already stacked against them simply because they championed the environment, they were Indians and they were poor. In truth, these people who fought 'the last fish war' had no choice in what they did. It was simply a matter of survival for the culture and the people who believed in it.

If there is any reward for what these unusual people did during their lives, it will be that they did something good, not only for those of their time but those who were destined to follow. Less than two dozen stalwarts of two rivers will always be remembered for what they did. Bob Satiacum and his two brothers Buddy and Junior, The Quinault [Clifford Mowich], Bernard Whitebear, Su'Zan Satiacum and a determined number of Puyallup, who fished upriver, could finally shed their status as criminals. They accepted the verdict from a court of law that would set them free. These comrades in arms who fought a difficult battle for years against great odds on the Puyallup River and Commencement Bay could now resume their natural ways of living.

On the Nisqually River, to the south, it was always Billy Frank Jr., Hank Adams, Don McCloud, Janet McCloud, Al Bridges, Maiselle Bridges, Suzette, Valerie and Allison Bridges. This valiant group aided by a small number of teenagers and small children were always in the forefront, ready to fight for their rights during those hectic and bitter fish wars on the water.

At one time, not that long ago, Billy and his people were considered renegades, even criminals, by the State of Washington. Today many people across the nation regard him and his people as heroes. For Billy and his tribal members, it was a battle worth fighting.

Thoughtful people now wonder who the criminals and renegades really were. Careful analysis must reveal that it wasn't the Indians who broke the law of the land, invaded, trespassed, assaulted, harassed and confiscated possessions owned by others. It was those who wore helmets, carried long nightsticks and had badges pinned to their jackets. It was also those in the Washington State Government, from the Governor down through the legislature and all the agencies below. These advocates must have believed in what they were doing, enforcing laws in the American way, laws that did not include or benefit those with a different colored skin or were native to the land.

The decades long fight of the Nisqually against great odds finally ended with the Boldt decision in 1974 when a small bit of justice was finally served.

10. Finis

TODAY THE PUYALLUP, the Nisqually and all the other tribes included in the Medicine Creek Treaty have survived those very difficult times. There were other clashes between the whites and Indians in other parts of the state but the main focus in this book is of the ferocity experienced by the Puyallup and the Nisqually for decades.

Since the days of Governor Stevens, there had never been any favorable legislation experienced by the Puyallup and Nisqually tribes until the Boldt decision. From those days in 1854 and after, the tribes have lost over thousands of acres of land, the right to survive and live in their natural way and the freedom to use the land unrestricted as they had for centuries. This harassment promoted by the white population increased over the years as their numbers grew. Over time it affected the tribe's practice of their cultural rights and the freedom to pursue their beliefs and religion unhindered.

Now many have scars, physically and emotionally, that bear witness to what the tribes went through during those trying times. During those days of fighting for their rights, the Indians never forgot who they were or why they were fighting. They struggled day by day for decades just to make it. They did it through strength of character and an unwavering belief that they were doing what their forefathers would have done.

The Puyallup and the Nisqually, always in the forefront, were the direct targets of the white authorities. But these people, native to the land, were secure in their thoughts that those of the past would be proud of their efforts to sustain and carry on what traditions were left to them.

Now that the fish war is over, there is finally peace among the two tribes. Those who want to can now devote themselves to a way of living that is natural to them. They can try to recapture a way a life that was disrupted and so important to themselves and their forebears.

Since the battle over fish has ended, new challenges surfaced that effected both tribes. With the origin of a bingo hall, then casinos, great amounts of money came to them. In the beginning, no one in the tribe had experience dealing with such matters. It took time for the Puyallup and the Nisqually to learn how to handle this new way of life. It took diligence and concentration for some to gain the confidence needed to cope in a different world. After over a hundred years of extreme poverty, forced upon them by the white man, it was difficult for some to face change.

Some adapted easily to the wealth that has come to them from new forms of business. Others would learn the importance of financial planning. Strong leaders would emerge to apply sound practices to the fast growing businesses that were unheard of only a short time ago.

Life today is better for the Puyallup and the Nisqually. With the advent of new business opportunities, they are making more money than anyone could have imagined. Because of this, some are living in the fast lane. For others in the tribe, it is almost too fast.

To a few in the tribes, the influx of large amounts of money is still a surprise.

The Puyallup and Nisqually are not greatly concerned by any negative thoughts of the whites now. They are too busy living their way, as best they can, in a new world open to them. Things are better now, since those bitter years of the 50s, 60s and 70s. During those times, no one ever thought about having money. All could only remember that there was never enough.

Now diversified investments in the Port of Tacoma and other forms of business are open to the Puyallup. It is difficult for some in the tribe to understand this new way of life. In time, the young Puyallup and Nisqually, armed with higher learning, will grow to take over and make the important decisions for the tribes.

All members can now afford food for balanced diets. Because of this they are healthier. The children of the past were not as fortunate. Some of both tribes, who had bad teeth, were ashamed to smile. They did not want to expose to others the cavities that discolored and riddled their teeth. They were extremely self-conscious. Today, because they can afford dental care, they are no longer reluctant to smile when times are good.

Children will not have to be absent from school and fall behind because of illness. Those in the tribes are now able to receive the healthcare that a deceitful government once promised and denied them. Today a beautiful new health clinic that displays Indian art and architecture has been built where the Cushman Hospital once stood; it provides complete care from optometry to dental to any Indian who needs it.

The Puyallup and Nisqually children now get the education they were once promised by a dishonest government within the borders of their own reservation. The young will no longer be sent to distant Off-Reservation Indian Schools where the policy of erasing Indian cultures of all tribes was stringently promoted. The Puyallup have already taken it upon themselves to build a new school on the reservation called The Leschi School that has an enrollment of nine hundred. Students that attend classes represent sixty-five tribes and are transported in from miles around.

Now parents are thankful they have enough money to buy their children shoes. They are grateful their children will no longer be self-conscious. The children will no longer be barefoot when they go out. They will no longer be ashamed to leave their homes wearing hand me down clothes, full of patches. Now there is enough money to tend to all their clothing needs.

With the Nisqually, advancements are more difficult to define. One has to look hard to see if any changes have occurred since they were invaded and mistreated by others. If anyone in the tribe has prospered since the difficult days, it is nearly impossible to measure. The numbers of the tribe have always been small and they have lived quietly in tune with nature in a remote part of the state. Visitors who come to visit their small reservation will see that it is still that way.

During the days of the fish war their neighbors, the Puyallup, had eclipsed the experiences of the tribe because of their size and location. The Nisqually had gone basically unnoticed by most whites until it was discovered their river was full of salmon. During their days of harassment, and afterwards, they carried on as they always have. They only take from nature what is needed and it is done in a serenely, almost religious, manner. The need to possess and accumulate more has never been a part of their ways.

The Wah He Lut School that sits near Frank's Landing, marks the only significant change on the tiny reservation. It sits quietly within numerous fir and cedar trees and is not imposing to the surroundings. Teachers and staff are polite and welcome visitors. The interior is immaculate and relates well with the exterior through large glass windows. It is obvious that the students are trained well and enjoy being a part of the building and the tribe itself.

As you enter the expansive foyer, the authentic fishing canoe of Billy Frank Jr. is positioned high from the ceiling; it can't be missed. There is only a fleeting memory of the violence that the grounds once experienced in the sixties at Frank's Landing. The artwork present there is a treasure; it is well worth a trip to view.

Later, another addition to the tribe's assets was the construction of the Red Wind Casino that is visited regularly by whites, maybe even the Sportsmen.

Because there are such great differences in the cultures of whites and Indians, it is unlikely that each will never completely understand, agree and accept the philosophies of the other. The religions of each are miles apart. Most whites believe in Christianity which deals with salvation in another life somewhere else. Admittedly, a number of Indians are now followers of the Christian faith. Somewhere along the line, they did not have the strength or the belief in their own native religion. Because of extremely hard times, they sought spiritual help in another way.

Those Indians who truly understand their religion still adhere to it. The Indian religion centers on 'mother earth.' It is revered and considered with respect. Those Indians have no need to seek other places for salvation. The idea of Indians seeking 'the happy hunting ground' is a myth, probably invented in Hollywood.

The impulses that drive each race are far apart. Whites have a need to acquire, control and change. They have been driven, probably for centuries, to satisfy these needs. One has to only study history to see and understand this. Indians of the past were satisfied with what they had and there was not a great need to have more. Now everyone, even a few whites, recognize this need to acquire simply as greed. With whites this could be attributed to genealogical impulses formed and honed for centuries in another way of life, in another place.

Differences in knowledge are also apparent in the two races. Those Indians who understand their culture find it unnecessary to search for more. Their ways were followed and adhered to for centuries by their forefathers. It was based on knowledge and practice acquired over hundreds of years that adhered to their environment. Some may have been because of instinct but it was certainly based on hard won experiences in understanding their environment and their everlasting quest to search for the truth.

When one searches for motivations that evolved into the clashing of cultures, the answers come easily. With the whites, there was a simple need to survive in a new and challenging environment. This led quickly to a need to conquer, replace and possess. What fueled the above was their belief that their way of life was superior to those who were native to the land. The whites felt that with the changing times all, white and Indian, would have to adjust simply to survive.

With the Puyallup and Nisqually there was a long-standing indoctrination of culture that was ingrained and too strong to dismiss. Since they had survived for centuries in their way of life there was no need to change. This was reinforced by the ability of their forebears to understand and foresee what was to come in the future.

With the Puyallup and the Nisqually they were forced to understand quickly the threats to their culture. They knew that with the loss of almost all of their land the only thing left for survival as a people was maintaining their right to fish in their accustomed places. They insisted this be a part of the Medicine Creek Treaty and as it turned out, this was their only Godsend.

Despite recent changes that favored Indians, most whites felt they were only temporary. In the long run, they felt the Indians had to change their ways simply to survive in a new world. The whites were aware there were too many people living in the area now to ignore this. They knew that as time went on, land would become scarce. Food, such as the fish that came from the water, would not accommodate those large numbers who now fished the waters, whether for food or sport. They felt it was just a matter of time when everyone, White and Indian, would have to change their ways whether they liked it or not.

Many whites believed that their resistance to Indian fishing was not due to racism or prejudice, but changes that were beyond the control of everyone. In today's world, there were just too many conditions and issues to deal with. Stepping back into history and trying to rectify age-old issues would not solve the problems that now faced both whites and Indians. Life was now moving too fast.

But hard feelings still remain. One night in the summer of 2004, Su'Zan Satiacum went to a 7/11 store on the eastside of Tacoma to buy some groceries and a cup of coffee. As she stood waiting to pay the cashier, a middle-aged white man approached and read the printed accolades to Bob Satiacum that appeared on the front of her T-shirt. The words immediately angered the man and he swore aloud and punched Su'Zan squarely in the face. She was stunned, but did not fall, as the man walked angrily to his car outside and drove away.

Su'Zan was sixty-three years old at the time; it was eighteen years after Satiacum had passed away. It was a good thing for that brave white man that it was not the year of 1965 when Su'Zan was a young, strong, determined lady. The result might have turned out differently. That night this incident gave indication that the clashing of cultures in the Tacoma area was still very much alive. It gave credence that as long as whites and Indians found it necessary to live next to each other and try to solve problems that neither side could understand or wanted to accept, the attitudes and behavior of each would change little.

One day, years after Satiacum's death, the Federal Way School District in Washington State thought it would be a good tribute to name a new middle-school after him. At first, many thought it would be a good idea to do this and honor a local Indian who might become legendary in his fight for Indian rights. But, once again, those who did not like Satiacum rose up and strongly challenged the idea.

Everyone was aware that he was charged with tax evasion. Others cited that he had molested a young girl in British Columbia, where he was hiding. Earlier, others had charged that Satiacum arranged for someone to be killed by a hit-man. Later, a number in the Puyallup tribe sided with Satiacum to clear his name of all charges. In time, these charges could never be proven and they were dropped. As time went on the move to honor him was set aside and then forgotten.

In the fight for their rights, The Puyallup and Nisqually were always guided by the age-old reasoning of their forebears and elders. On the other hand, whites would continue to carry on their beliefs that they came from a superior race that was ordained to rule and control.

It would be years before anyone would appreciate the contributions of Indians to the world in general. For centuries, whites had been indoctrinated that Indians were a backward race and not on the same par as those of the western culture.

In William A. Betts's book *Essays on Native Americanism*, the author examines the contributions in governance, medicine, pharmacology, architecture, agriculture, astronomy and mathematics. Betts points out that no one book could cover it all; the contributions are so vast and extensive it would take volumes to cover them. This book, and others like it, should be in every school, every library and every bookstore in the nation. If accurate knowledge of the history of this continent, as it deals with Indians is the goal, then books such as Bett's should be read and understood by everyone.

Prior to the writing of this book, few in the United States, Indian or white, had much comprehension of the contributions of Indians to the world stage. Whites in this country have always underestimated the achievements of Indians. Most would die of old age before they understood the depth or agree with what Indians had to offer. They would spend a lifetime in ignorance of the first people of this continent and the contributions they have made.

Whites invented what they consider history. Those who wanted their writing to reflect favorably on their own kind authored such material. Much of history was not studied and based on truth. The accomplishments and deeds of whites were greatly exaggerated. If anyone wanted to know the truth of white heroes of the past they would be astonished by their findings. They would find that their heroes were not such fine people after all. Those interested would discover that Hollywood had accomplished a fine face-lift on most of them. Once Bernie Whitebear was asked what he thought of the courageous deeds of Americans fighting at the Alamo. Bernie answered with a shrug, "At that time, if there had been a back door to the Alamo no one today would have the damndest idea of what you're talking about."

For years, the history books in the schools of this nation have promoted falsehoods about Indians that were based on misconceptions, distortions and downright lies. Most of the important contributions of Indians had been glossed over or totally omitted. The authors of this verbiage did not want their readers to know the truth, beauty and depth of the Indian culture. They did not want to convey conceptions that Indians might be, at least, partially civilized. Furthermore, they did not want the reading public to be aware of the continuous crimes their forefathers had committed against Indians throughout their time on the North American continent, as they killed, stole, polluted and raped the land.

Fortunately after decades, history books of today are more accurate and inclusive of Indians and their unique way of life. In 2009, the Lake Washington School District in the state of Washington adopted a new Social Studies series for elementary and junior high students entitled 'History and Cultural Studies'. Textbooks in this series included:

Early Northwest Coast People by Margit E. McGuire, PhD,
Pacific Northwest Native American History: The People of Cascadia by Heidi Bohan
The Wampanoags and the First Thanksiving by Margit E. McGuire, PhD
History and Government, the Oregon Trail by Margit E. McGuire

In more than one case these publications state the truth, without compromise, of the abuses committed by whites against Indians in the past. Hopefully a new generation of whites who study this material will be further advanced than their forebears.

After decades of poverty and strife inflicted on the Puyallup, the Nisqually and other tribes who depended on the salmon for their survival things were changing. A quiet and thoughtful man in Washington D.C. arose to fight in his unique way the distressing problems all Indians in the United States faced. In the 100th Congress, Senator Daniel Inouye of Hawaii assumed the chairmanship. Under his post, the committee held more hearings and reported more legislation to the full Senate than any other committee. Landmark legislation encompassed more than a dozen acts concerning Indians from Indian healthcare to self-determination, from education assistance to Indian land consolidation. These acts were presented and passed for the benefit of all Indians in the United States.

Senator Inouye was an individual who believed in justice and, without question, became the most influential person in the Senate in Washington D.C. Unlike others in the nation's capitol who wanted to be in the limelight, this great man did it quietly without fanfare. Before that, he was the most courageous hero of World War 11, winning a host of medals for his bravery in combat against the Germans. Finally, after fifty years, a biased congress reluctantly awarded him the Medal of Honor.

Afterwards, Senator Daniel Inouye of Hawaii, with the help of Senator Patty Murray of Washington State, championed the Indian Gaming Regulatory Act and other important legislation which opened new avenues for many Indians to change for the better their lifestyles. This allowed them to finally escape the harsh and demanding realities of poverty and racism that had been endured by all Indians for over a century and a half.

Because of Senator Inouye's concentrated and continued efforts on behalf of Indian people, new types of mechanical wonders, for lack of a better name, have now been invented that are willing to set things right. These wonders do not spend time trying to belittle or harm others but they are certainly out to get what it feels is their fair share. Observers might view these devices as liberal, but no one knows for sure.

The design of these apparatus,attracts a new breed of whites who probably, without knowing it, provides generous offerings to the Indians of today. At all times of the day and night anxious whites, driven by an undeniable purpose, leave their cars parked in an overcrowded lot; they make their way, with joyful expectations, toward an immense building. They sometimes walk great distances just to get inside. It is no fun during the rainy season when the cold wind is blowing and a storm is brewing.

Once inside, some sit most of the day and into the evening smoking one cigarette after another, putting hard earned cash into these brightly colored BUT NOISY CONTRAPTIONS. ONE MIGHT GUESS, THESE OBJECTS MADE OF PLASTIC, steel and whatever else was designed and manufactured by other whites, . After spending hours emptying their pockets of every cent they own, the whites learn that these unusual inventions, continually emitting outrageous noises and glittering, disturbing lights, waits patiently to consume more.

As one customer exits, another comes, to sit and play, gleeful and confident of huge earnings. But, alas, these wonderful devices have no favorites. Upon studying them, one might conclude that they have descended and inherited their self-centered traits and behavior from some preceding generation.

A few of the customers who are a bit historically minded have vague remembrances of manifest destiny in the 19th century when their forebears seemed to be in control. But what is happening now seems to be somewhat in reverse. Nevertheless, no one knows for sure so the customers search for a place to sit hoping this will be the time when their luck will change and they will reap huge wins.

From the beginning the machines were flanked by hundreds just like them, in a crowded, noisy room.. But the brightly lit and colorful machines are not that concerned with history. They seem to be at home there as they wait patiently for one customer after another, eager to try their luck. The machines seem inert, feigning a state of sleep; but once a customer approaches and comes within range and inserts a coin, they jump to life and roar greedily as they prepare to voraciously gobble up everything the customer holds dear including the last sawbuck, rarely giving anything in return.

However, there are times when the machines feign generosity and allow the customer to win back meager amounts. The devices seem to be in good spirits and gracious, but no one knows for sure. Nevertheless, this reaction is nothing but a ploy. They are designed to encourage the customers to dig deeper into their pockets and play more. But even as the customers exit their favorite casino, unsmiling, with empty pockets and in a state of confusion and disappointment, plans are already being made to return and try once again.

Dan Inouye, US Army captain, was the recipient of the Congressional Medal of Honor for the important part he played in World War II. He later became a US senator representing the state of Hawaii. He championed the Indian Gaming Regulatory Act and other legislation that opened new avenues for improving the lives of American Indians. Courtesy: Daniel Inouye Institute, Hawaii

> "There has been, what we feel, to be a shameful effort to paint a picture of the Indian as deliberately wasteful and greedy of the resources. When we hear that we are destroying the fish, we resent it. I can't tell you how deep our feelings are. It's like telling the Plains Indians they destroyed all of the buffalo."
> – James Jackson: (Quinault Tribal President)

Acknowledgments

I MUST THANK THE FOLLOWING PEOPLE for making this book possible. In the beginning, Bob Satiacum shared stories of his young life, his teen age years and finally his adventures on the Puyallup river and beyond. I first met him in 1951 and grew to be totally impressed by his courage and commitment to the cause he believed in. He was a unique man among men and we were friends until he died in 1991.

Billy Frank Jr. was another friend whom I admired greatly. His treatment by white authorities, when he was only a young boy, turned me to disgust. I was awed by his discipline and sense of duty to nature and his fellow man. His religious statement of life convinced me he knew more of those most important issues than any priest, preacher, or for that matter any pope.

This was followed by the memories of a great fisherman, the Quinault (Clifford Mowich). His experiences and adventures in Tacoma and Commencement Bay add greatly to the writings of the book. He was a man of deep thought that was always laced with humor. I fished with him on the Puyallup River for six months in 1957 and found him a unique fisherman, dependable, and full of hard won knowledge. I always found his understanding and philosophy of life unique and full of zest.

Later, Janet McCloud, the Tulalip, provided information of the conflicts endured by Billy Frank Jr. and the Nisqually on their tiny reservation and the Nisqually River that sustained them. Janet was a real warrior, committed to her beliefs and undaunted by the enemies she faced. She was the first director of the Survival of the American Indian Association (SAIA). Janet was always there when needed, always ready to fight for what she believed in. She is, without question, the most outspoken Indian I have ever met.

163

Alongside Janet McCloud's efforts Hank Adams an Asinaboin-Sioux, ably led the National Indian Youth Council (NIYC) and later the Survival of the American Indian Association (SAIA). Because of his efforts to organize Indian protests and coordinate publicity, several non-Indian organizations eventually came to support the Puyallup and the Nisqually goals. Adams success at doing this proved extremely valuable to the Indians in winning their war over the fish and finally setting up the trial that took place in 1974.

The continued fight for rights of the soft spoken Al Bridges and his family must be noted. The harassment over the years by the white authorities failed to stop him and his family from fishing the Nisqually River as they always had. They were always there and never intimidated by the large numbers representing the fisheries of Washington State. This held true when they were attacked and beaten viciously in 1965, by these intruders, on their own land.

The information provided by Bernard Reyes (Whitebear) adds another dimension to the book as it tells how Satiacum became an important mentor to his overall growth and inspired him to accomplish many notable victories and receive dozens of awards during his lifetime. He fished with Satiacum for over seven years and afterwards he and I had a number of conversations of the fish wars, always reaching the same conclusions.

Su'Zan Satiacum is another warrior. Her stories and adventures bring the book full circle. She has to be admired for her bravery, efforts and the abuses that befell her to help the Puyallup and the Nisqually people. She faced treacherous odds during her lifetime and was injured a number of times in her people's fight for justice.

Bob Peterson's contribution cannot be dismissed. His photography adds a personal touch to this book as he experienced firsthand Marlon Brando's visit to Tacoma and Su'Zan Satiacum's skill as a driftnet fisher. As a professional photographer on assignment for Life Magazine and Seattle Magazine, he provided a number of important photos that complement this story in a very special way.

Bob Morrisson, once again, has been very important in providing excellent quality to old photographs. If a 'picture can tell a thousand words,' then I have to thank Bob for his contributions to this book and his willingness to always do more.

John Love performs his own type of magic with his computer skills. He was able to locate images and information needed that would definitely take thorough understanding to find.

The Last Fish War is the fourth book published, beginning with *White Grizzly Bear's Legacy, Bernie Whitebear,* and *B Street.* If Therese Kennedy Johns had not been the editor, they would not have reached completion, and I would probably still be working on the first one.

Other important contributions to the publishing of this book were made by the following individuals who helped in the acquisition of significant photographs.

Willie Frank, the son of Billy Frank Jr.
Tony Meyer of the Northwest Indian Fisheries
Larry Workman of the Quinault Tribe
Carolyn Marr, Mohai Librarian
Teresa Wong, the daughter of Harry Wong
Harry Wong, the son of Harry Wong
Sara Daly Hamakawa, Daniel Inouye Institute
Hank Adams, Asinaboin-Sioux (NIYC)

PERSONAL INTERVIEWS
Malcolm MacLeod
Janet McCloud
Billy Frank Jr.
Myrtle Satiacum
Su'Zan Satiacum
Robert Satiacum
Buddy Satiacum
Junior Satiacum
Bernie Whitebear (Bernard Reyes)
The Quinault (Clifford Mowich)
Chester Wong

LITERARY RESOURCES

Barsh, Russell L. *The Washington Fishing Rights Controversy: An Economic Critique*. University of Washington, Graduate School of Business Administration, 1977.

Betts, William A. *Essays on Native Americanism*, Nashville, Tennessee, 2009

Grant, Lindsey. *Too Many People*. Seven Locks Press, 2000.

Hefferman, Trova. *Where The Salmon Run. The Life And Legacy Of Billy Frank, Jr*. Washington State Heritage Center & University of Washington Press, 2012.

McCloud, Janet and Casey, Robert. "The Last Indian War." Bulletins No 29 and 30.

McEvers, Charles L. *Uncommon Controversy*. University of Washington Press, 1970.

McLuhan, T.C. *Touch the Earth. A Self-Portrait of Indian Existence*. Outerbridge & Dienstfrey, 1971.

Nerburn, Kent, Ph.D and Mengelkoch, Louise, M.A. *Native American Wisdom*. New World Library, 1991.

Reyes, Lawney. *Bernie Whitebear. An Urban Indian's Quest for Justice*. University of Arizona Press, 2006.

Sherman, William. "Case # 9225339 Suzan Satiacum." Seattle Magazine February Vol 23, 1966.

Wilkinson, Charles. *Messages from Frank's Landing*. University of Washington Press, 2000.

NEWSPAPER ARTICLES

"A Resource Divided." The Seattle Times, Nov. 10, 1996.

"Rest in Peace, Billy." The Seattle Times, May 7, 2014.

"The Puyallup Tribe and the Salmon Nations." The Vashon Loop, March 10, 2015.

CPSIA information can be obtained
at www.ICGtesting.com
Printed in the USA
LVOW03*1732051216
515850LV00002BA/3/P